D1395025

THE PEAKY BLINDERS

COMPENDIUM

THE
PEAKY
BLINDERS

COMPENDIUM

HODDER &
STOUGHTON

First published in Great Britain in 2021 by Hodder & Stoughton
An Hachette UK company

1

WITH THANKS TO MATT WHYMAN

Peaky Blinders™ © 2013-2021 Caryn
Mandabach Productions Ltd.

Peaky Blinders is a registered trademark of
Caryn Mandabach Productions Ltd.
Licensed by Endemol Shine Group.

All rights reserved. No part of this publication may be
reproduced, stored in a retrieval system, or transmitted, in any
form or by any means without the prior written permission of
the publisher, nor be otherwise circulated in any form of binding
or cover other than that in which it is published and without a
similar condition being imposed on the subsequent purchaser.

A CIP catalogue record for this title is
available from the British Library

Hardback ISBN 9781529347579
Paperback ISBN 9781529347722
eBook ISBN 9781529347739

Designed by Nicky Barneby, Barneby Ltd
Typeset in Harriet Text by Hewer Text UK Ltd, Edinburgh
Printed and bound in Great Britain by Clays Ltd, Elcograf S.p.A.

Hodder & Stoughton policy is to use papers that are
natural, renewable and recyclable products and made
from wood grown in sustainable forests. The logging and
manufacturing processes are expected to conform to the
environmental regulations of the country of origin.

Hodder & Stoughton Ltd
Carmelite House
50 Victoria Embankment
London EC4Y 0DZ

www.hodder.co.uk

CONTENTS

Key:

 Big Ideas

Style

Faces

Life

Places

Food & Drink

ANARCHY IN THE UK

'The good old cause!'

The call to reject all forms of authority and state control took shape in the ancient world. Deriving from the Greek word *anarchos*, which means 'without authority', anarchy as a philosophical idea spread in popularity across Europe and America throughout the nineteenth century. As a political force, it began to gather ground at the turn of the twentieth century.

At a time when the Peaky Blinders made capital with their business ambitions, anarchism emerged in Britain. It took the form of a hard-left movement committed to tearing up the establishment by any means and constructing a society based on cooperation, mutual aid and the belief that everyone is equal. Anarchists drew support from the working classes to radical thinkers and anti-establishment idealists.

In *Peaky Blinders*, it is Ada Shelby's lodger, James, who playfully expresses an enthusiasm for the anarchist movement. The young man strikes Tommy as a dreamer rather than an agitator, and yet he knows that the wider world considers anarchists to be a threat to society. Tommy duly plays this fear to his advantage by persuading James to accompany him to Alfie Solomons' bakery, where he asks him to wait outside. In order to secure his safe exit following the meeting, Tommy informs Alfie that his associate has been instructed to trigger a grenade he planted in the bakery on the way in. He describes James as 'a professional' anarchist, and likens him to a group behind the infamous and deadly Wall Street bombing of 1920.

Ultimately, it's enough to convince Alfie that Tommy's accomplice will do whatever it takes to cause chaos as a catalyst for change.

It could be said that anarchy in the UK reached its height as the Peaky Blinders expanded their business interests from Small Heath to racecourse ownership and black-market export. In some ways, the movement was largely absorbed throughout the first half of the twentieth century by left-leaning political movements as well as by wider world events, such as the 1917–23 Russian Revolution and the Spanish Civil War, 1936–9. As a symbol of establishment resistance, however, anarchist ideals remain a powerful means of seizing attention. The spirit of the early twentieth-century anarchists can be seen in everything from the punk rock movement of the late 1970s to Reclaim the Streets in the 1990s and the radical environmentalism of today's Extinction Rebellion protests.

ARROW HOUSE

'Every night since the funeral, he comes back in the morning to see Charles and feed the horses. When it gets dark he goes off again.'

When Tommy Shelby takes up residence in his grand countryside estate, it's a far cry from his humble beginnings in a terrace on Watery Lane. The red-stone mansion with its stained-glass windows offers him respite from the pressures in his life, and a place for him and his new wife, Grace, to start a family. Later, as a widower with his son, Charlie, Tommy's prized property serves to remind him of what he's lost. As his sister, Ada, observes, the house becomes a painful place for him to be. With servants' quarters, grand staircase, ornate ceilings, imposing fireplaces and long dining table, it just seems cold and hauntingly empty. Arrow House is not a place without drama, however. Throughout the story of *Peaky Blinders*, it's the scene of pivotal events from a mass arrest of the Shelby family to a staging of *Swan Lake* that's attended by British fascist leader Sir Oswald Mosley and interrupted by a shooting.

Many of the Arrow House scenes in *Peaky Blinders* are filmed at Arley Hall and Gardens, which is one of the most prominent family-owned stately homes in the north-east of England. Built between 1832 and 1845 by the landowner, Rowland Egerton-Warburton, the mock Elizabethan hall stands on the site of the original building, which dated back to 1469.

Arley Hall is located over fifty miles north of Birmingham, just outside Northwich in Cheshire, and is open to the public. With its grand approach and handsome front, the house and gardens are no stranger to our screens, having also featured on the *Antiques Roadshow*, *Coronation Street* and numerous other productions.

 ## ASYLUM FOR THE INSANE

'If he's caught they won't hang him on the grounds of insanity. He will go back to the same place I found him. He'll just have had a very eventful holiday, which he will probably believe never really happened.'

In his attempt to take down Oswald Mosley, Tommy recruits the help of an old war comrade, Barney

Thompson. In the years since his return from the frontline, the former sniper has struggled with 'shell-shock' and manic episodes. Tommy finds him incarcerated in a dimly lit and windowless asylum cell. Conditions are bleak for him; effectively a reflection of society's attitude to mental health at the turn of the twentieth century.

The concept of a lunatic asylum is difficult to comprehend today, as is the terminology used to describe those considered to be 'mad' or 'insane', who – until the later years of the twentieth century – were often locked up in institutions for a lifetime on the grounds that families and communities needed protecting from them. This was frequently open to abuse, with 'difficult women' sometimes finding themselves committed against their will, along with those suffering from what we now understand as dementia.

By the 1920s, shortly before Tommy helps Barney to break out, Britain's asylums housed almost one hundred thousand inmates. Each institution was legally bound by the Lunacy Act of 1845 to employ a qualified physician to care for the patients. Treatment was often minimal, however, with the emphasis on keeping large numbers of inmates calm, occupied or under control. By the 1930s, at a time when asylums had become increasingly underfunded and overcrowded, leading psychiatrists also developed and promoted more extreme, invasive treatments in the form of electroconvulsive therapy and lobotomies. It was only with the development of effective drug treatment in the 1950s, combined with a more humanitarian and socially inclusive approach to mental health issues, that such institutions finally began to close their doors for good.

BETTING SHOP

'That's my brother Arthur's office ... down there's my brother John's office ... that's where we slate the runners and the riders.'

Horse trainer May Carleton does her level best not to look surprised at what she finds on her tour of the 'gambling den' at Tommy Shelby's invitation. It certainly commands attention at first sight. Earlier, when Tommy first opens a side entrance hidden behind curtains in the family's neighbouring house in the terrace at Watery Lane, it reveals a whole new world next door. With rooms knocked through and front windows boarded to keep out prying eyes, the neighbouring space forms the heart of the Shelbys' thriving business interest. Here, in this noisy confine choked with cigarette smoke, Tommy, Polly, Arthur, John and their workforce chalk up odds on horse races around the country and take money from hopeful punters.

What May finds is a betting shop, buzzing with activity and completely illegal.

Gambling in the early twentieth century was a popular pastime. Over the preceding three hundred years, it had grown to appeal across the social spectrum. Wagers took place on everything from horse racing to card games, cock fighting and bare-knuckle fighting. It was a means of displaying wealth for the upper classes, and an escape or entertainment for the workforce.

Concerns about the social effect of gambling existed back then as they do today. The Gaming Act of 1845 attempted to deter the practice by giving the punter no legal protection should the bookie refuse to pay out. Later, the Betting Act of 1853 restricted the practice to licensed pitches at racecourses. In effect, this outlawed what we would consider today to be high-street betting shops. Neither Act dampened the thirst for gambling. If anything, they encouraged sharp practices and drove the business underground, which is why the Shelbys operate their Watery Lane venture with a lookout stationed at the front door.

THE BILLY BOYS AND BILLY FULLERTON

'They run every man in every coal mine and on every shipyard in East Glasgow. Ties with Belfast, UFV. Protestant razor gang. They also dabble in politics. Y'know. Muscle for fascist rallies.'

When Arthur Shelby learns that Michael had encountered the Billy Boys on his return voyage from America, his description of their activities is delivered with a sense of foreboding. Arthur is well aware of the gang's ruthless reputation, spearheaded by leader Jimmy McCavern, who sets out to challenge the Peaky Blinders on several fronts. While McCavern is a work of fiction, the outfit he fronts is drawn from underworld history.

In the 1920s, street gangs in Glasgow were fiercely territorial. In the city's East End, where Irish immigrants had settled in the preceding century, they were also divided along sectarian lines. Here, Catholic gangs such as the Tim Malloys and the Norman Conks pitted themselves against their Protestant rivals including the Calton Tongs and, arguably the most notorious outfit of all, the Brigton Billy Boys.

Hailing from the city's Bridgeton (or 'Brigton') district, the Boys chose their name in recognition of the seventeenth-century Dutch Protestant monarch, William of Orange, ruler of Scotland, England and Ireland from 1689 to 1702. William has fondly been referred to as 'King Billy' by many Protestant Scots and Northern Irish ever since his victory at the Battle of the Boyne in 1690. The gang was led by a one-time shipyard worker called Billy Fullerton. Dubbed the 'Razor King', Fullerton had risen through the ranks as a vicious street brawler and racketeer to govern – at its height – an 800-strong gang that was virtually a small army. The Billy Boys dressed in a uniform of suits and 'doolander' bonnets, and regularly marched into Catholic territory singing songs proclaiming their strength and superiority. Clashes were frequent and often brutal, which only strengthened Fullerton's reputation across the city.

At a time when British media interest in the underworld was focused across the Atlantic on Al Capone, Billy Fullerton was portrayed as a Glaswegian Scarface. In 1932, he even wrote a long article for *The Weekly News* about gang life. Though professing to have reformed, Fullerton was later involved in a provocative sectarian march in Belfast. He went on to join Sir Oswald Mosley's British Union of Fascists, and organised security at its meetings. As a gang, the Billy Boys went into decline during the 1930s, and effectively disbanded with the onset of the Second World War and compulsory military service. Fullerton died aged fifty-six in 1962.

BIRMINGHAM

'I've heard very bad, bad, bad things about you Birmingham people.'

The second largest city in the UK, located in the West Midlands, Birmingham forged much of its character in the early twentieth century as a manufacturing powerhouse. 'The City of a Thousand Trades' evolved from a hub of small enterprises to become a centre for engineering, metalworking and automotive industries. A network of transport links by rail and canal fuelled the city's growth, and indeed the Peaky Blinders capitalise on the considerable waterway network to expand their business interests. By the time Tommy reaches London, for a meeting with Alfie Solomons at his Camden bakery, it seems his gang has forged a reputation back home that precedes them.

In bringing the city and the era to the screen, *Peaky Blinders* creator, Steven Knight, drew from the childhood recollections of his parents and wider family. The factories were a source of light, fire and hammer blows, as well as black ash that floated down to carpet the cobbled streets and rooftops. The working classes lived in cramped conditions, trapped in pockets of slums that wouldn't be redeveloped until after the Second World War. It was the pubs that offered a respite from this unforgiving life, where the boozy atmosphere saw plots hatched and dramas play out.

BIRMINGHAM SMALL ARMS COMPANY (BSA)

'It was meant to be routine ... I'm guessing my men were drunk.'

When Tommy orders his men to steal a crate containing motorcycles, only to find they've accidentally come away with a consignment of Lewis machine-guns, it could have only come from one factory in the city: BSA.

The Birmingham Small Arms Company was founded in 1861 as a manufacturer of machine-tooled weaponry. The owners – primarily gunsmiths – created a large factory in Small Heath, home of the Peaky Blinders. Despite winning big contracts in the early years, the company was forced to diversify in the late 1870s and duly went into the bicycle-making business. This might seem an odd switch from an outside point of view, but the machines built for the manufacture of guns were easily adapted to produce large quantities of low-cost and standardised bike parts.

As the century turned, the company survived by carefully balancing bike and arms production, as well as taking steps into the motorcycle industry. BSA proved to be a fruitful source of employment for local people, and a vital contributor to the local economy. Demand for munitions soared during the First World War, of course, dropping off considerably after Germany and the Central Powers conceded defeat in 1918. One year later, BSA responded by setting up a subsidiary company dedicated to the production of bicycles and motorbikes. In *Peaky Blinders*, this draws the attention of an ambitious young street gang leader and explains the mix-up that pits Tommy against Chief Inspector Campbell and his men.

As a company, BSA was known for acquiring businesses as well as diversifying. It acquired Daimler as well as the Lanchester Motor Company in order to make use of the latter's factory next door, though neither automotive manufacturer proved hugely successful in its hands. Nevertheless, BSA's core work – the manufacture of guns – continued to grow. During the Second World War, with sixty-seven factories under its wing, the company is thought to have produced over half the small arms used by England in the conflict. Following Germany's defeat, BSA refocused its attention on bikes and motorcycles, and became an industry giant on acquiring Triumph Motorcycles in 1951. Towards the end of the decade, however, a downturn in fortunes forced the company to begin offloading its major interests – with Raleigh acquiring the bicycle division. By the early 1970s, a succession of sell-offs and takeovers effectively reduced BSA to a marque. As the business was absorbed into outside ownership, an important chapter in Birmingham's history as the workshop of the world came to a close.

THE BLACK PATCH

'Thomas, should I go and speak to Queen Mary Lee?'

Today, Black Patch Park is a twenty-acre green space to the north-west of Birmingham's Jewellery Quarter. Located in Smethwick, it's bordered by a railway line, an allotment and industrial buildings. Over one hundred years ago, the area was effectively just a dumping ground for furnace waste known as 'the Black Patch'. A bleak and barren pocket of land, it was also home to a community of Romani Gypsies and provides the source of an intriguing story about a star of the silver screen.

In recognition of their Traveller heritage, the Shelby family, in one *Peaky Blinders* episode, gather at the Black Patch to pay their last respects to John. Just as the body is considered a vehicle for the soul on earth, so in Gypsy folklore the vardo (wagon) is regarded as a vehicle for the body. This meant that when a member of the community passed away, the wagon was regarded as having served its purpose and ceremonially burned. At John's funeral, his body is laid to rest inside the wagon – along with his treasured belongings – before it's set alight.

John's wife, Esme, has a strong connection with the Black Patch. It's home to the Lee family, who have a close bond with the Shelbys due to the couple's arranged marriage.

When Tommy's plans to expand the business into London come under fire, Esme offers to recruit foot-soldiers by visiting the community and speaking to the appointed head, Queen Mary Lee. In reality, from the late nineteenth century to the early twentieth century, the Black Patch was home to Romani Gypsy royalty. King Esau, and his queen who survived him by just a few years, commanded fierce loyalty from the families who camped on the grounds. They claimed that Travellers had been granted the right to live there, having faced growing persecution when roaming country lanes before effectively being forced onto land regarded as useless by the authorities. Despite the conditions, the Romani people thrived here into the early twentieth century. There is even some evidence, in the form of a letter found by his daughter Victoria, after his death, to suggest that the great entertainer, Charlie Chaplin, was born in a caravan at the Black Patch in 1889. Whatever the truth behind this claim, there is no doubt that this unassuming space is rich in Gypsy history, folklore and legend.

BOLSHEVISM AND THE RUSSIAN REVOLUTION

'I want to borrow a book ...'

When Tommy Shelby's secret wetwork for Winston Churchill brings him into contact with the exiled aristocrat, Grand Duke Leon Petrovich Romanov, along with his wife and niece, the influence of Russian events on the story of the Peaky Blinders deepens. Having dealt with communist sympathisers like Freddie Thorne, Tommy now finds himself dealing with once-powerful but still well-connected figures. As a man who likes to be prepared, Tommy visits Ada at the London library where she works in order to carry out background research on an ideology and uprising that shook the world.

The Grand Duke and his family, living in luxury in London's Wilderness House courtesy of the British establishment, are involved in a plot to smuggle tanks into Georgia. This is part of a secret plan to overthrow the fledgling Soviet Union, established by the Bolsheviks in 1922 as part of the Russian Revolution.

The Bolsheviks – which means 'majority' in Russian – were a Marxist political force led by Lenin. They were effectively the largest faction of the Russian Social Democratic Labour Party, which believed in communist rule. In 1917, fired by what they perceived as vast social and economic inequalities, the Bolsheviks seized power in Russia. During the revolution that followed, which lasted for six years, they brought down the monarchy and ruling classes, forcing wealthy and aristocratic figures such as the Duke and his family to flee, in order to establish the Russian Soviet Federative Socialist Republic. The name was later changed to the Communist Party of the Soviet Union, which maintained power until the system collapsed in 1991.

In 1924, one year after the end of the Russian Revolution, exiles like Grand Duke Leon Petrovich Romanov remained fiercely hostile towards the Bolsheviks and contemptuous of the Soviet framework of government they installed. The Bolsheviks were often known as 'The Reds', which was the main colour of the Soviet flag, and a loose force of allies determined to overthrow them were called 'The Whites'. In *Peaky Blinders*, Tommy is tasked with stealing tanks and smuggling them out of the country for the pro-capitalist Whites. Preparing for the heist, he realises he is caught up in a shadowy establishment plot to blow up trains on British soil and frame The Reds for this. The resulting international incident would provide the government with a seemingly legitimate reason to confront the Soviet Union and what it considered to be the communist threat. With this in mind, Tommy sets about playing the two sides to his own advantage.

BOOTS

'My brother would be wiping bits of you off his boots by now if I wasn't preaching caution.'

In the early twentieth century, the working man required footwear that was fit for purpose. Boots were a popular choice for many, and not just because jobs were often labour intensive. We only have to look at the state of Watery Lane to appreciate why people needed something sturdy on their feet. In an industrial age, with poor drainage and horses remaining a popular choice of transport, the streets were effectively paved with soot, grime and muck.

As they rose to prominence, the Peaky Blinders were noted not only for their caps, complete with a razor blade stitched into the brim, but for their equally distinctive boots. Ankle height, in heavy-duty black or tan leather – often decoratively perforated or brogued – and with a practically indestructible sole, these were designed to look good and last a lifetime. As Tommy warns the factory owner, Mr Devlin – as Arthur broods behind him – they can also be used to do some damage.

The kind of cap toe boots sported by Tommy and his brothers in 1919 feature an Oxford-style closed lacing system. They're hand-stitched and sometimes welted, which involves cementing a durable strip of leather or rubber between the upper and insole. After the First World War, many ex-soldiers simply kept their military boots to wear on civvy street, while those who could afford it purchased lighter boots with more flexible uppers. These were usually worn for clerical or office-based work. They also became more popular as leisure wear during the 1920s, while facing stiff competition on the fashion front from the leather shoe.

BOW TIE

'Fuck what they think.'

Arthur doesn't stand out from the Shelby family just for being the first into a fist fight. When suited and booted in the Peaky Blinders uniform, it's his bow tie that really sets him apart from his brothers. Such a traditionally formal item might be at odds with Arthur's hot-headed character, and yet in different ways both pack a punch.

The bow tie has its origins in the seventeenth century. It evolved from a simple scarf worn by Croatian soldiers to bind their shirts at the neck, which then became the cravat beloved of the ruling classes. The garment we recognise as a bow tie today emerged in New York in the late nineteenth century. It was quickly adopted on both sides of the Atlantic as a simple but distinctive fashion statement. While the standard necktie was growing in popularity at this time, many came to see the bow tie as an unfussy alternative. Physicians were said to prefer them, for example, because they didn't dangle in the way when operating on patients.

By the time Arthur Shelby's name started to inspire both fear and respect across Small Heath, the bow tie had become far less commonplace than the standard tie, though in some ways this just made the bow tie wearer look even more distinctive. The 1930s saw a revival and reinvention of this idiosyncratic item of attire as women adopted what had been an exclusively male preserve, but it was Winston Churchill who arguably made the bow tie his own. The bow tie's popularity may have declined since the end of the Second World War, but today it remains the perfect accompaniment to the tuxedo and ideal for anyone who shares the same uncompromising spirit and fearless streak as the eldest Shelby brother.

Bow tie basics

CLIP-ON
For anyone with no time to stand in front of a mirror fussing, the clip-on bow tie is quick to fit – attaching to the front of the shirt collar – and completely level if that's the look you choose.

PRE-TIED
The pre-tied version comes with a neck strap, hidden beneath the collar, keeping it firmly in place.

SELF-TIE
There's nothing more satisfying that tying a bow tie yourself. Variations include the butterfly and batwing, which describe the shape of each blade, or the single-end bow tie. The fact that all varieties of the self-tied bow tie sit naturally off-kilter is considered to be a mark of authenticity, so adjust for comfort without feeling you need a spirit level to finish the task.

HOW TO TIE A TRADITIONAL BOW TIE

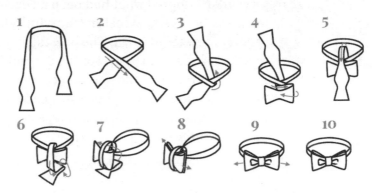

1. Place the tie around your neck, with one end an inch longer than the other.
2. Cross the long end over the short end.
3. Tuck the long end up and under the short end to form a neck loop, and then drop the long end over your shoulder to keep it out of the way for a moment.
4. Take the short end, pull it across the collar and form a bow on one side.
5. Drop the long end over the neck loop, which will form the centre of the bow.
6. Holding both lengths in place, fold the long end into another bow.
7. Take the bow formed by the long end and tuck it through the neck loop behind the short end.
8. Gently pull each bow to form a knot.
9. Adjust each end until both sides are even and the bow tie is secure in place.
10. Step out with confidence.

BOWLER HAT

'A gentleman would take off his hat and put out his pipe.'

A man like Chief Inspector Chester Campbell represents the establishment. When he's not in a topper, what hat embodies this more than the bowler? Complete with a heavy overcoat and cane, this is a man dressed to uphold his belief in justice, decency, discipline and respect at all costs. Polly Gray might be affronted that he doesn't remove it when entering a church, but Campbell is a man who also chooses to defy convention when it suits him. In this case, as a staunch Protestant in a Catholic place of worship, he keeps the bowler on his head as a simple means of needling a Peaky Blinder in prayer.

A hard felt hat with a low crown and rounded brim, the bowler first came into existence in London in 1849, created by the London hat-makers Thomas and William Bowler. At the time, the top hat was the popular choice. The bowler, however, proved to be a smart, hard-wearing and practical alternative that was less likely to be dislodged on the move.

Initially, the bowler appealed to the working classes, before finding a place with office-based workers at the turn of the twentieth century. The preferred option of insurance brokers, bankers and clerks, the bowler in Britain became shorthand for 'everyman' – a look that celebrated compliance and convention over individuality. For a figure like Chief Inspector Campbell, tasked with stamping out rebellion, it was the perfect choice of headwear.

BOXING

'If a man wants to set his stall up with fellows lamping each other, he needs himself a licence.'

Arthur has only paid a visit to the underground boxing venue because the promoter, Mr Marston, failed to request permission from the Peaky Blinders. Then he discovers that one of the fighters in the ring is his father, back from America in search of funds. After the bout, Arthur Shelby Snr invites his eldest son to sit down and discuss business, artfully conjuring a proposition that will ultimately fleece the family. In this dimly lit warehouse, as the pair discuss plans over a drink with young Finn in tow, another fight can be seen taking place in the background. A crowd has assembled behind the ropes, and as with the bout before it, the gloves are off.

Bare-knuckle boxing, or prizefighting, had been a feature of British life since the late seventeenth century. It was a dangerous, bloody and popular pastime that only saw gloves become a feature (see **Queensbury Rules**) with the introduction of regulations for amateur championships. While bare-knuckle boxing was never illegal, by the turn of the twentieth century this often-brutal variation was considered to exist on the fringes of the law. The inherent dangers are evident when Arthur loses his self-control during an ungloved training match and pummels his young opponent to death.

Following the First World War, organised boxing in the UK became a hugely popular sport. Men returned fighting fit from the frontline and boxing clubs sprang up around the country. Money naturally followed, and it's this that draws Tommy's interest in promoting Aberama Gold's son, Bonnie, when he proves to be a natural in the ring. Bonnie's big fight versus Goliath, represented by Alfie Solomons, sees the Peaky Blinders taking bets from the moment the doors open and punters flood the great hall. Then, as now, boxing for many was a compelling and often lucrative spectacle.

BREAD

'We bake the white bread. We bake the brown bread. We bake all sorts ...'

It's been a staple food through history, and is a source of solace as well as sustenance in *Peaky Blinders*. Polly Gray leaves a loaf in her basket of provisions outside Ada's door, hoping to coax out her heartbroken niece – who has recently given birth to a baby – in the wake of Freddie Thorne's arrest. Later, when getting reacquainted with Michael, her long-lost son, Polly lovingly makes him sandwiches to take with him on his first outing with his cousins. Then there's the moment Chief Inspector Campbell inspects the tongue-and-pickle offering from Sergeant Moss with the kind of reverence reserved for a work of art. Bread-making is nowhere in evidence when Alfie Solomons first leads Tommy on a tour of his beloved bakery, but if the Jewish gangster hadn't been using it as a front for rum production you can be sure his loaves would be second to none.

In short, and as a reflection of its importance in the Peaky Blinders era, bread is a simple, everyday food that cuts across class and appeals to both upholders of the law and the underworld.

As the First World War deepened, following its outbreak in 1914, food became increasingly scarce. Government campaigns encouraged people to cut down on certain items. With imported wheat becoming a precious commodity, posters appeared imploring the population to 'eat less bread'. Rationing didn't finish until 1920, two years after the end of the war, but attitudes prevailed. As the Peaky Blinders begin to expand their business enterprise, people tended not to waste food. They appreciated what they had, which included basic provisions.

While the government focused its efforts on protecting and maintaining the supply of wheat for industrial bread-making, it also encouraged people to bake their own. With ingredients at a premium, hard to come by or even unavailable, new and inventive recipes began to circulate that helped to bulk out the loaf using such additions as potato, cooked rice or soya. After the war, as the troops returned home and key ingredients became more readily available, bread became more popular than ever before.

1920s bread

Bake your own vintage loaf and taste a slice of the
Peaky Blinders life

INGREDIENTS

- 500 grams of flour
- 1 tablespoon of fat (butter or lard, but to go fully
  authentic use chicken fat or clarified beef fat)
- 1 teaspoon of sugar
- 1.5 teaspoons of salt
- 7 grams of yeast
- 300 ml warm water

METHOD

1. Pour half the flour into a bowl.
2. Add the fat and salt.
3. Dissolve the yeast in a small amount of the water
   and then add to the mix.
4. While stirring, add the remaining flour and water
   to create a dough.
5. Knead the dough on a floured surface until firm.
6. Leave to rise for two to three hours in a warm,
   humid environment.
7. Pre-heat the oven to 210 °C/420 °F/Gas Mark 8.
   Place the loaf in a large, greased bread tin and bake
   for 20 to 25 minutes until the crust turns golden
   brown.

THE BULLRING

'All repressed female workers welcome.'

It's a familiar meeting place for the people of Birmingham, with a history that dates back to the twelfth century. In *Peaky Blinders*, the Bullring serves as a rallying point for a walk-out by female workers over equal pay and rights led by union activist, Jessie Eden. The passion behind her principles even speaks to the women at Shelby Company Limited. Led by Linda Shelby, they leave their posts to join a protest in a show of strength.

Located in the heart of the city, opposite St Martin's church, the Bullring exists today as a major shopping centre. Just over nine hundred years ago, what was an open space served as a corn market. During this period, bull-baiting was often carried out in public before the animals were slaughtered for meat. It's believed the bulls were tethered to an iron ring, which ultimately led to the market area becoming known by the name it retains today.

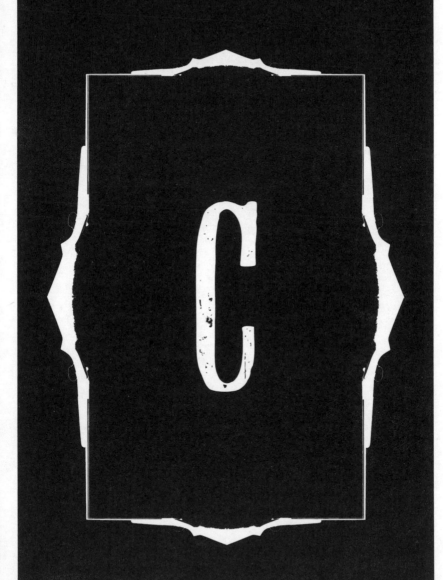

CAMDEN TOWN

'What business do you have in Camden Town, Tommy?'

Home to Alfie Solomons' operations, Camden in the 1920s was a thriving transport hub for both rail and waterway. Effectively a gateway for goods from the north into London and the Thames ports, the town's Regent's Canal dock was a magnet for warehouses and factories. While the railways would eventually draw all trade away from the longboats, the canal proves to be strategically important to Tommy Shelby in *Peaky Blinders*. When Charlie Strong enquires about his reasons for travelling there, Tommy reveals he's expanding his business interests from the Midlands to the south.

CAP

'Your uniform? Terrifying, I'm sure.'

Nothing distinguishes a Peaky Blinder more than the rounded hat with a small, stiff brim pulled over the brow. Stories through the generations suggest members of the original Birmingham street gang concealed a razor blade in the brim. While some uncertainty remains concerning this, it makes for a powerful and enduring mythology. Chief Inspector Campbell might pour scorn on Arthur's choice of headwear on interrogating him, even when he uncovers the blade, but there's no doubt it places a nasty weapon within easy reach for the Shelby brothers and their associates.

In the nineteenth and early twentieth century, the flat cap became a popular form of headwear for the working-class man. It was usually made from cloth material, with tweed or cashmere creeping in as the upper classes adopted the cap for leisure pursuits such as driving or shooting. In the TV series, the Peaky Blinders wear a variation of the flat cap. With a slightly fuller body, it's often known as the 'baker boy' or 'news-boy' cap, and is made from six to eight fabric panels that converge under a button at the top.

Mystery surrounds how the original Peaky Blinders earned their name, but one cap-related theory is that with the peak pulled low they could hide their identity. Whatever the case, the cap has become a timeless accessory for every class of gentleman.

CAPITAL PUNISHMENT

'In the bleak midwinter ...'

The first recorded cases of capital punishment in Britain date back to the fifth century. By the time Arthur and John Shelby, and Michael and Polly Gray, face the noose for murder, having also been convicted for sedition and sabotage, the practice had become a grim mainstay of the penal system.

Up until 1868, death by hanging was conducted in public and often attracted large crowds. When public execution went behind prison doors, just a handful of witnesses were required by law, such as the prison governor and chaplain. Final words were customary, and for his Arthur cites the opening lines from a Christina Rossetti poem popular among soldiers during the First World War. The words serve as an enduring source of comfort to the Shelbys in harrowing times – even if the quote does prove mercifully premature when the four executions are commuted at the last minute. In 1965, Parliament temporarily suspended capital punishment in the UK, before formally abolishing the practice in 1969.

AL CAPONE

'We also contacted a businessman in Chicago . . .'

It's a name that inspired both fear and respect across America throughout the 1920s and 30s. When Polly and Tommy reveal that the Peaky Blinders are in business talks across the Atlantic with the infamous crime boss, Al Capone, it leaves Luca Changretta, the New York mobster who has travelled to England to avenge his father, momentarily lost for words.

Alphonse Gabriel Capone was born in Brooklyn, New York, in 1899. His criminal activities began at an early age when he joined the Five Points Gang, whose members included fellow Italo-American hoodlums such as Lucky Luciano and Johnny Torrio. During his time in the Big Apple, Capone got into a fight at a brothel and suffered a knife injury. The wound swiftly earned him the nickname that would reinforce his status as a formidable crime figure: 'Scarface'.

In 1919, Capone followed Johnny Torrio – who had been working for a syndicate boss named 'Big Jim' Colosimo running gambling and brothel rings – to Chicago. In the same year, responding to a call for temperance from religious groups, the American government banned the manufacture, sale and transport of alcohol. The Prohibition era, which lasted until 1933, resulted in a huge demand for booze on the black market. Colosimo refused to get involved in bootlegging, which led to a rebellion in the ranks. Capone is believed to have been involved in Colosimo's assassination so that his old associate, Torrio, could assume control of the organisation.

Torrio's position at the top came to a premature end following his arrest in 1925 for running an illegal distillery. When Capone took over, he showed a flair for public relations that was arguably ahead of his time. While everyone knew he made his fortune through racketeering, the mobster worked hard to present himself as a man of the people who sought to improve the lives of the people of the Windy City.

Away from the flash of the press photographers' bulbs, Capone ran 'the Outfit', as his mob was known, with ruthless efficiency. On 14 February 1929, this culminated in one of the most notorious acts of gang war retribution when seven members of a rival mob were gunned down in cold blood. The Valentine's Day Massacre, as it became known, began to turn the tide of public opinion against Capone and sparked the beginning of his fall from power. Despite his involvement in everything from prostitution to protection rackets, federal law enforcement agencies struggled in vain to make charges stick. Capone did short spells of prison time for contempt and carrying a concealed weapon, but ultimately his downfall was sealed in a mundane but watertight way. In 1931, having lived an opulent lifestyle with no apparent means, Al Capone was sentenced to eleven years for tax evasion.

Much of Capone's sentence was served at Alcatraz, America's most notorious federal jail on an island in San Francisco Bay. Prison did little to blunt his formidable reputation, yet on his release in 1939 the former mob boss emerged as a shadow of his former self.

During his time inside, Capone was diagnosed with advance syphilis, a sexually transmitted infection he had picked up as a younger man. As a result of the effect of the disease on the brain, his mental capacity was judged to have been severely diminished. A free man, but considerably incapacitated, the infamous kingpin retired to Florida, where he died in 1947 following a cardiac arrest aged just forty-eight. Although his life was relatively short, Al Capone's reputation endures as the embodiment of the American gangster.

CATHOLICISM

'I wish to confess ...'

Religion plays a central role in Polly Gray's life. For her, the Catholic Church is a place of comfort as much as confession for the life she leads. Whenever Tommy needs to speak to his aunt, he frequently finds her in contemplation before the altar with her rosary beads in hand. Raised as a Catholic alongside his brothers, Tommy is familiar with the rituals of the faith. When the sinister Father Hughes enters the Peaky Blinders story, dominating Tommy through blackmail and violence, he forces him at one point to recite the Act of Contrition. That Hughes demands

Tommy directs the prayer towards him, instead of God, is in character for a man who also appears to abuse his position of authority in the priesthood in other ways.

Like Polly, many UK Catholics in the early twentieth century were related to Irish immigrants who had sought to escape from poverty – notably the Great Famine of 1845–52. In search of work and a new life, the greatest numbers were to be found in industrial ports and cities, with Birmingham formally becoming a diocese in 1911. The city's Catholic community would continue to grow through the century, largely thanks to immigration from countries such as Poland and Italy.

CAVIAR

'I recommend the teal and the pork. Though your guest I'm sure will order the caviar.'

Considered a delicacy around the world, caviar consists of a salt-cured roe from the sturgeon family of fish. When dining at The Ritz with Grand Duke Leon Petrovich Romanov, Tommy sits across the table and watches him greedily devour a generous serving with cream, as predicted above by the *maître d'*. Russian caviar was regarded as a premium in the early twentieth century, though much of the world's supply at that time was in fact exported from America.

It's worth noting that the Grand Duke uses a non-metallic spoon to load his bread with caviar. Connoisseurs recommend utensils made from mother-of-pearl, glass or even gold, as metal is said to impinge on the purity of the taste.

CHAMPAGNE

'I think tonight you should not drink vodka with your champagne.'

In the world of *Peaky Blinders*, champagne is the drink to toast accomplishments and is poured at high-society events. Tatiana and her Russian uncle and aunt gladly quaff it like water, Polly orders a glass while earning disapproving glances for being an unaccompanied female at the bar, and Grace presents Tommy with a bottle to mark her contract of employment as a book-maker for Shelby Company Limited. By the early twentieth century, champagne had acquired the social cachet that it holds today. Despite the drink's growing popularity, however, the champagne industry faced significant supply challenges during the era due to several mildew outbreaks in the first ten years of the century – blighting the grape harvest – and then the upheaval of the First World War. The conflict had a particular impact on the champagne regions of north-east France, where many celebrated vineyards were lost. By the time the Peaky Blinders rise to power, however, the champagne is flowing once again and savoured with every toast.

BRILLIANT CHANG

'Mr Thomas ...'

When Tommy receives a panicked call from Finn, who tells him there's a gun to his head, he realises that the man who arranged it – currently sitting across from him in a fur-lined coat – is a strategic thinker. It also means the proposal Tommy has just heard from the infamous Chinese businessman cannot be ignored.

In *Peaky Blinders*, Brilliant Chang seeks to recruit Tommy and his men to help in a bold opium-smuggling operation. The character of Chang may seem like a notable invention, but in fact it is based on a notorious drug dealer of the age, whose life is wreathed in mystery.

Brilliant (or Billy) Chang was born in Canton in 1886. He came to England in 1913, opening a Chinese restaurant in Birmingham. In 1917, Chang moved to London. The previous year, due to rising concerns about alleged drug misuse among troops, the law concerning substances such as cocaine, opium and heroin had been tightened somewhat. Despite possession requiring a medical prescription, the appetite for such substances remained high, especially on the socialite scene.

Sensing an opportunity, and forging connections, Chang soon earned a reputation as a prolific dealer. Charming and charismatic, he reportedly built up a loyal female clientele. This was also his undoing following the death of Freda Kempton, a twenty-one-year-old dance instructor, from a suspected cocaine overdose in 1922. For, during the inquest, a friend of Kempton's testified that Chang had supplied her with the drug. Although the coroner ruled that her death was due to 'suicide whilst temporarily insane', he viewed Chang's claim to innocence in the matter as dubious. The court also acknowledged a lack of sufficient evidence to bring charges, yet Chang would be forever associated with her death.

The police kept a close eye on Brilliant Chang, sensing he had something to hide, which impacted on his business. In 1924, after a drug addict pointed the finger at him as a dealer, a raid on his flat in Limehouse uncovered a quantity of cocaine. Chang was immediately arrested and charged.

At Chang's trial, accounts emerged of a man who hosted wild sex and drug parties. The press sensationalised the story, calling on ethnic stereotypes to portray him as a shadowy and scheming criminal mastermind who preyed on innocent girls. On being found guilty, Brilliant Chang served a fourteen-month prison sentence before being deported in 1925. From there on, despite considerable media interest, his story slips into a fog of uncertainty.

It was reported that Chang had moved to the European mainland and established himself as the continent's underworld drug lord, while claims also surfaced that he had lost his sight due to excessive narcotics use and was holed up in Hong Kong. There is even some suggestion that the man himself spread this latter rumour to divert attention from his real whereabouts. The only certainty is that Brilliant Chang had effectively spirited himself away from the spotlight of attention, which is why his appearance in the Garrison comes as a surprise to Tommy and Arthur in more ways than one.

CHARLIE CHAPLIN

'I bet you've never heard Charlie Chaplin speak.'

When Tommy escorts Grace to a cocktail party in London, rather than the picture house she's expecting, she's stunned to see the silver-screen legend across the room. Intent on impressing her, Tommy explains that the bodyguard accompanying Chaplin is a Romani Gypsy who once had links in Birmingham. He also reveals that Chaplin shares the same Traveller heritage, but 'keeps it a secret'.

What's most striking about this fictional scene is that everything Tommy shares with Grace is based on fact. In real life, Chaplin's bodyguard, Wag McDonald, was an underworld associate of Billy Kimber. Wag and his brother, Wal, headed the Elephant and Castle Mob, who formed a working allegiance with the Birmingham Boys.

In 1921, Wag fled the country following his implication in a brutal gang fight called the Epsom Road Battle. Later that decade, he moved to the City of Dreams to set up a business providing security for film stars. One such client was Charlie Chaplin, arguably the most famous movie star of the age, who appointed Wag as his personal minder.

In the same year – that in which the *Peaky Blinders* scene takes place – Chaplin had travelled by ship from America to England to promote his movie, *The Kid*. It was his first return to his native shores, Chaplin having left to pursue an acting career in 1913. Now, as one of the most recognised faces in the world, his presence attracted huge crowds even when he attempted to slip away to visit childhood haunts in south London.

No birth certificate exists to validate Chaplin's claim that he was born in Walworth in 1889. All that's known is that as a child he experienced great poverty and hardship. Charlie's mother, Hannah, separated from her husband, struggled with psychological issues. Charlie had an older half-brother, Sydney, who lived with his father, but the boys didn't meet for some time. Unable to adequately support her youngest son, Hannah sent Charlie to live in the workhouse on two occasions before he turned nine.

Chaplin's parents both had backgrounds as music hall entertainers, and he would soon follow in their footsteps. For Chaplin, the stage offered a temporary escape from the real world, and his talent as a performer who could connect with his audience was quickly recognised. Aged fourteen, with his mother sadly committed to a mental asylum, young Charlie signed with a theatrical agent in London's West End. Building on his reputation as a magnetic young performer, he joined his half-brother in a touring company. When he was in his early twenties, the company dispatched a small group on a tour of American vaudeville halls, where Chaplin began to show star potential. In 1914, he signed a contract with the New York Motion Picture Company, and set about developing the tramp character that would make him one of the world's first global celebrities.

In 1991, fourteen years after Charlie Chaplin's death aged eighty-eight, the late actor's daughter discovered a letter in a locked desk drawer. It was written by an acquaintance of Chaplin's father, accusing him of covering up his Gypsy roots. He alleged that Chaplin's mother, Hannah, had in fact been living in a wagon at the Black Patch when she gave birth to him. The claim has never been proven, though it's believed Chaplin might have been mindful of the potential stigma of being associated with Romanies and chosen to keep it from public record. In recognition of the likelihood that the great entertainer had hidden his Gypsy roots, Chaplin's son, Michael, unveiled a memorial at Black Patch Park in 2015 that commemorated the community's association with the site.

SIR WINSTON CHURCHILL

'I really must come up to Birmingham someday and spend an evening with your family. They sound interesting.'

Tommy Shelby and Sir Winston Churchill hail from opposite sides of the tracks. When they first come into each other's lives, via Major Campbell's efforts to strengthen law and order in Birmingham, one is the head of an underworld organisation and the other is a secretary of state. In fact, Churchill is initially at peace with the fact that Campbell intends to dispose of the Peaky Blinder once he has carried out a secret mission for the crown. It's only when this rising politician recognises how useful Tommy can be that he orders him to be saved from execution at the hands of the Red Right Hand. Despite the vast differences between them, a mutual respect exists that bonds the two men, so that they come to rely on each other.

Of all the historical figures that have inspired characters in *Peaky Blinders*, Sir Winston Churchill is perhaps the most prominent as the wartime prime minister who helped to defeat the Nazis. In real life, there is no suggestion that he had early connections with a street gang leader like Tommy Shelby, but though the narrative departs from Churchill's career in several places it reflects his involvement with wider world issues.

Winston Churchill was born in 1874 at Blenheim Palace in Oxfordshire, and spent his early years growing up in Dublin. After school, military college, then a period in the army and as a war correspondent, Churchill entered Parliament in 1900 as the Conservative MP for Oldham. With a strong commitment to social improvement, Churchill left the party in 1904 to join the Liberals. By the end of the decade, married with the first of four children (one of whom would die young from sepsis), he was serving in the cabinet as president of the Board of Trade.

Promoted to First Lord of the Admiralty in 1911, Churchill played a central role in modernising the navy, only to resign from the post during the First World War over the disaster at Gallipoli in 1915–16. Here, a large-scale sea landing by the Allies led to an eight-month coastal siege in which a quarter of a million troops lost their lives. Churchill returned to serve in the army for the remainder of the war, seeing action on the Western Front at the same time as the Shelby brothers in their Peaky Blinders back story.

After the war, Churchill served in David Lloyd George's government. He was the Secretary of State for War from 1919 to 1921, responsible for the massive demobilisation operation to bring the troops home, before becoming Minister for the Colonies until 1922. It's during this period in *Peaky Blinders* that the character of Churchill appoints Chief Inspector Campbell to track down the army-issue machine-guns and becomes familiar with the name of Tommy Shelby.

In 1922, Winston Churchill lost his seat at the General Election – while also becoming disillusioned with Liberal Party policies – only to return to government in 1924 under the Conservatives as Chancellor of the Exchequer. By 1929, when his *Peaky Blinders* character comes face to face with Tommy Shelby, Churchill had become an opposition back-bencher once more following Labour's victory at the General Election that year. Tommy himself is a Labour MP in the storyline, and this sees Churchill pay considerable interest to the fact that he's come to the attention of another character inspired by a real-life figure, Sir Oswald Mosley.

Winston Churchill was opposed to fascism in all its forms, though some critics also argue that he held what could be considered problematic colonialist views. After a relatively quiet decade in public life through the 1930s, in which painting became a central passion, he returned to government and ultimately the seat of power just after war had broken out with Germany. Churchill remained prime minister throughout the Second World War, overseeing Hitler's defeat in 1945. Despite losing the General Election that year, he would become prime minister for a second time in 1951. Considered to be one of the most significant wartime leaders in British history, Churchill received a knighthood in 1953 for his service to the nation. At his death in 1965, at ninety years of age, Sir Winston Churchill was given a state funeral.

CHINATOWN

'Hurry up or they will kill us all!'

In the opening scene of the very first episode of *Peaky Blinders*, a man shepherds a young girl through a narrow market passage spiked by daylight. Oriental banners and lanterns hang overhead and sheets dry on lines. It could be Shanghai, but is in fact a cramped pocket of Birmingham in 1919. Here, Mr Zhang runs a laundry and brothel, while it's his daughter, Mei, who has been summoned by Tommy to perform a public 'fortune-telling' on a racehorse.

Chinese seafarers were the first to settle in Britain in the early 1800s. Small communities with distinct identities began to grow in major ports like Liverpool and London. This was further strengthened by the work of the East India Company, which imported goods such as cotton, silk and spices from the Far East. In Birmingham, the Chinese immigrant population remained very small until after the Second World War. Today, the city's thriving Chinatown area can be found opposite Birmingham New Street Station.

CIGARETTES

'I am chosen? OK. Can the chosen one smoke?'

There is no moment in Tommy Shelby's life that is seemingly unsuitable for him to moisten a filter end between his lips before lighting up. Even when faced with IRA representatives who would sooner put a bullet 'in this scum tinker's head', he does so. At any time, no matter what the threat, this is a man who keeps his cool by reaching for the cigarettes.

Smoking was commonplace in the early decades of twentieth-century Britain, largely sparked by the development of mass production of cheap, pre-rolled cigarettes in the late nineteenth century. The tobacco industry marketed smoking to men as well as women, pitching it as an equal-opportunities habit in the wake of the Suffrage Movement. Both Tommy and Polly are often seen drawing their cigarettes from portable silver cases, which protected the contents and were also regarded as a mark of sophistication at the time.

The link between smoking and health issues was largely unexplored until the late 1920s. The filter-tipped cigarette was invented in 1925. Considered to be a means of reducing the potential for harm, it did not gain widespread popularity for many years, until the 1960s.

Tommy Shelby's cigarette of choice is Sweet Afton, which was an Irish unfiltered brand launched in 1919 made from Virginia tobacco. The name is taken from the first line of a poem by Robert Burns, whose image features above a rural landscape on the front of the packet. Production of the brand ceased in 2011.

 ## CLOCHE HAT

'What do you think?'

Women's fashion in the 1920s was modern, sophisti-cated and diverse, and yet when it came to headwear – as Lizzie Starke knows on presenting herself to

Tommy at the Epsom races – just one style of hat crowned them all: the cloche.

Borrowing the French word for 'bell', which neatly describes its shape, the cloche was invented by a Parisian milliner, Caroline Reboux, and popularised by stars such as Josephine Baker and Joan Crawford. Often made from felt, the hat was designed to be worn close to the head with a soft brim at the front.

Worn by everyone from Polly Gray and Ada Thorne to May Carleton, Lizzie and Linda Shelby, the cloche hat was wildly popular across Europe and America throughout the decade. It has gone on to retain a time-less quality that combines elegance with confidence: two qualities embodied by all the female players in the Peaky Blinders world.

COCAINE

'Sometimes, when we boys are feeling blue, this is what we do . . . it's called Tokyo.'

It's the youngest Shelby brother, Finn, who gives Arthur his first introduction to a drug that almost proves to be his undoing. As the Roaring Twenties took off, the white powder that Finn taps out on the table from a small, blue glass bottle intended for snuff rapidly became associated with living the high life. He calls it by a slang name, 'Tokyo', which may well have derived at the time from the cockney rhyming slang for 'nose' (Tokyo Rose), and suggests to Arthur it'll help to lift his mood. Sure enough, by the time the pair arrive for the reopening of the Garrison, Arthur is visibly wired and excitable. From London nightclubs to society circles, the drug responsible – more commonly known as cocaine – was regarded as an illicit but very fashionable party drug that chimed with the extravagant spirit of the age.

Throughout the nineteenth century, cocaine had enjoyed a reputation in Britain as a wonder drug with medicinal properties. Before its association with dependency issues was properly understood, and the law evolved in response, the drug was a key ingredient in treatments for everything from pain relief to syphilis, hay fever, seasickness, asthma and dysentery. In many ways, this gave cocaine an air of legitimacy when it started to be used recreationally in the early years of the twentieth century.

Attitudes towards the drug only changed during the First World War following what became known as 'The Cocaine Panic'. In the early years of the conflict, thousands of Canadian troops were stationed in Britain on their way to the frontline. A scandal broke out when a drug haul was discovered at a Canadian military camp. When the suppliers were arrested, breaking up a cocaine ring that used Soho prostitutes to sell the drug to the soldiers, it led to a sensational tale in the media of drugs, vice and moral decay. With stories circulating that over four hundred Canadian soldiers had been identified as hopeless addicts, cocaine became considered as a threat to the war effort by a general public fearful of a German victory. Shortly afterwards, emergency legislation was introduced to control the drug, along with opium, which had also attracted lurid, xenophobic headlines about the small but growing Chinese immigrant community. In 1920, both substances were prohibited along with morphine under the Dangerous Drugs Act.

By the time Arthur risks becoming derailed by cocaine, followed by his wife, Linda, as well as Michael Gray during his time in America, the risks associated with misuse of the drug were becoming recognised. It's Tommy who reminds his older brother that cocaine is a stimulant used to 'dope horses', and he later takes Arthur to task for cooking the books at the Eden Club to cover for his outgoings on the habit. Although Tommy might seek escape in opium, his concern about cocaine potentially causing his older brother to lose his self-control affords him a dim view of the drug.

COLLAR

'I will have a maid gather the buttons and sew them back on.'

A smart shirt forms part of the Peaky Blinders' signature look – even though Arthur tears his open in angry compliance with Tatiana's request to inspect his skin for tattoos – but it's the choice of collar from the period that adds true style and flair.

In the early twentieth century, a neckline revolution was underway in the world of men's fashion. During the late nineteenth century, the stiff, detachable collar had been commonplace, largely because men couldn't afford many shirts in their wardrobe, and as it was the collar that quickly got dirtiest, it was easier and more economical just to whip it off for washing. After the First World War, however, soldiers returned home with a preference for a softer, less starchy garment without the fuss of adding a collar. This relaxation of style was met with some resistance in established society.

In particular, it made the integral collar a symbol of modernity and rebellion, which should be perfect for a street gang intent on a razor-sharp look to match their attitude. It's just that Tommy Shelby is a man who likes to keep people guessing about his true intent.

As the Peaky Blinders emerge as a force to be reckoned with, Tommy steps out in either an integral or detachable collar. It's a nod to the rules, and also to his ability to rewrite them. With a range of different styles available, Tommy often favours a penny or club variety. This rounded collar is smart but relaxed, and works on its own or with a waistcoat and suit.

At those times when Tommy Shelby's work calls for a detachable collar, which he often removes after the job is done and before pouring a glass of whiskey, the collarless shirt alone is a look in its own right. Also known as a 'grandad' shirt, and with Irish origins like the man himself, it comes with full-length buttons or in a tunic style with buttons from the chest up. In addition, there are two types of collarless collar. The simple 'band' encircles the neck, while the 'mandarin' sits a little higher and is separated at the front. Tommy Shelby and his brothers are no stranger to either style, with or without a detachable collar. Even on those occasions when a shirt with an integral collar is called for, the Shelbys combine smartness and simplicity with devastating effect.

COMMUNISM

'Do they sit at home, comfortable with their full belly, while you scrape to find enough to put shoes on your children's feet?'

As a social movement, communism in Great Britain came to the boil in the early twentieth century. The 1917 Russian Revolution was regarded as a source of inspiration for many who believed that all class structure should be abolished, with the workforce taking shared ownership of the means of production. At a time of deep divides between rich and poor, and with soldiers returning from the war feeling disillusioned and unrewarded by the quality of life back home, it's no surprise to learn that the communist ideology attracted impassioned disciples such as Freddie Thorne.

As a union leader, Thorne attempts to disrupt factory output by inciting strikes among the workers. Following the Russian Revolution, there's no doubt that tensions were running high about the possibility of a similar communist takeover in countries across Europe. While British communists felt empowered by events, forming their own party in 1920, it coincided with the rise of the Labour Party, which attracted union backing and drew more moderate socialists away from the cause.

At the 1923 General Election, which led to Labour forming a minority government, the Communist Party of Great Britain stood four candidates but won no seats. While support ebbed and flowed for almost fifty years, the party always occupied the fringes of British politics until disbanding in 1991 after the dissolution of the Soviet Union.

CUFFLINKS

'The Peaky Blinders are here . . .'

As a matter of practicality, the cufflink became commonplace in Britain in the late 1800s. As shirts evolved, becoming stiffer through starching, so a simple button wasn't enough to secure the shirt sleeve. It required anchoring on each side by two linked studs or plates, and with so much creative potential a style trend was born.

With the Shelbys seeking to establish themselves as gentlemen, despite their underworld interests, it's no surprise that they are seldom seen without an under-stated but stylish pair of accessories to keep their shirt sleeves in place. On the dancefloor at Epsom, Tommy's impeccable appearance draw's Billy Kimber's attention before his eyes fall on Grace. A pair of solid, shining cufflinks can signify everything from good fortune to a heavy conscience, so choose wisely when it comes to a pair that embody your personality.

DEPARTMENT STORE

'And since we're celebrating, I had this delivered ...'

When Grace Burgess presents Tommy with a bottle of champagne to toast her contract of employment with Shelby Company Ltd, she tells him it came from Rackhams. In 1919, anyone who lived in Birmingham wouldn't fail to be impressed by the name.

Established in 1881 by John Rackham and William Matthews, this was a retail store with a difference. Instead of offering a specific range of consumer goods, such as haberdashery or ironmongery, Rackhams divided its considerable floor space into different sections such as haberdashery, millinery and dresses. The first department store, as it was known, was opened in Pall Mall, London, in the late eighteenth century. Harding, Howell & Co. catered mostly for female customers, who were drawn to shopping safely in one place. Others quickly followed, with department stores becoming an established feature of most major cities in Britain by the end of the nineteenth century.

In 1955, Rackhams was purchased by Harrods, which was subsequently acquired by House of Fraser. Rackhams was rebranded as House of Fraser in 2000.

DRESSES

'If I'm meeting a king, I won't be wearing a cheap dress.'

In the 1920s, Western fashion for women enjoyed a golden age. Elegance and simplicity combined with lighter, looser clothing compared to wardrobes in the late Victorian and early Edwardian era – which favoured high waistbands, long skirts and blouses. A rising awareness of women's rights fuelled an air of freedom and celebration, which meant this was the decade that celebrated the female form. Higher hemlines and bare arms became a fashion feature, and this shaped the dress styles of the decade.

We first enter the world of *Peaky Blinders* in 1919, of course. Our introduction to the family matriarch, Polly Gray, finds her dressed formally in a dark belted jacket, long, hobbled skirt, and scarf. It's an outfit more in keeping with time gone by, but that changes with the fortunes of the family. Later, her suits extend to a bold, daring three-piece, with gloves and aviator glasses. Having run the business while her nephews fought in the war, Polly is a woman in charge who also knows how to dress for pleasure.

From weddings and soirées to a sitting for her portrait, Polly Gray chooses evening dresses and gowns so light they practically float. There is something of the *femme fatale* about her, with a glint of sequin in the chiffon silk, a fox-fur stole over her shoulders and a cigarette never far from her lips. As the Jazz Age begins to creep in at the edges towards the late 1920s, Polly embraces the style with beaded headbands and fringed dresses.

By contrast, Grace Burgess chooses simple outfits and lets colour make the statement. She arrives in Tommy's life wearing green, symbolising her Irish roots. Following a negotiation for the price of a dress, she accompanies Tommy to a day at the races in red as the romance develops. Later, Grace chooses a lilac wedding dress for their marriage, a colour associated with mourning in recognition of the fact that she lost her first husband to suicide. Ultimately, Grace meets her own death in a neutral dress. It's intended to showcase the stunning emerald necklace presented to her by Tommy, who is unaware that it's been cursed.

Dress to kill
Classic womenswear from the Peaky Blinders era.

SKIRTS AND BLOUSES
A departure from the Edwardian one-piece dress, women began to wear long, high-waisted skirts, stockings and a billowing, tucked-in blouse shortly after the end of the First World War. By 1919, such an outfit was commonplace, accessorised with a scarf or necktie and ankle-high, lace-up boots.
As worn by: Polly Gray

EVENING GOWN
By the mid-1920s, dress designers recognised that women liked to dance. The hemlines rose, necklines plunged and the back was revealed in daring cuts guaranteed to draw the eye.
As worn by: Lizzie Shelby, Linda Shelby and Gina Gray

CHEMISE DRESS

A short, sleeveless design that hangs straight from the shoulders. Loose-fitting at the waist, this was a simple, popular style of evening dress that required little accessorising to make an impact.

As worn by: Ada Thorne

FLAPPER DRESS

As the stock market made gains along with women's rights, 1920s dress fashion also reflected the confidence of the decade. Straight, slim chiffon dresses, revealing both cleavage and calf, defined the 'flapper', which was a term used to describe women determined to make the most of their newfound liberties despite disapproval from the older generation. They wore lingerie instead of corsets, and accessories such as beads, bangles and headbands that encouraged creative expression, using everything from gemstones to ostrich feathers.

As worn by: Princess Tatiana Petrovna and Polly Gray

THE ECONOMIC LEAGUE

'Mr Shelby, I haven't finished with you yet ...'

When Tommy Shelby is tasked with stealing tanks to smuggle out of the country as part of a covert bid to help Georgian rebels overthrow the Bolsheviks in Tbilisi, he finds himself in a deep state drama of the age.

Tommy's shadowy handlers in the operation, who stop at nothing to ensure that he delivers the goods, are known by a number of names such as the Oddfellows, the Vigilance Committee, Section D and the Economic League. Represented by Patrick Jarvis MP and the paedophile priest, Father Hughes, this powerful, well-connected group play like puppet-masters behind the scenes of British politics.

Like so many storylines in *Peaky Blinders*, the dark forces that conspire to sacrifice the Shelbys to achieve their ultimate aim have some roots in reality. Every name that the group is known by can also be found in obscure realms of espionage, summary justice and fraternal organisations, but one stands out above them all.

In 1919, an influential group of right-wing business-men founded an organisation that set out to monitor and disrupt what they regarded as a growing threat from left-wing agitators and communist groups. The Economic League gathered information on principal players, keeping records on known communist sympa-thisers and applying pressure on various employers to blacklist them. The group organised meetings across the country to counter perceived threats to capitalist society, notably the 1926 General Strike, and sought to influence articles in the British press to reflect its members' views. The Economic League survived until the 1990s, when media investigations called their blacklisting activities into question.

JESSIE EDEN

'Then I'll be blunt . . .'

When a female trades union activist meets Tommy Shelby in the boardroom, her sheer tenacity and force of will in defending the rights of the workforce become clear from the moment she stands her ground.

It's 1925, and in the wake of the Russian Revolution – with the communist system installed – Transport and General Workers representative Jessie Eden reminds the Shelby Company boss that across the country there is a similar appetite for change among the workers. Tommy has just cut wages, which is a provocative move through Eden's eyes. He's also well aware that she's capable of standing up to factory owners, having led female workers across the city in a walk-out the previous year in their fight for equal pay. As Linda had encouraged Polly, Esme, Lizzie and the Shelby Company women to down tools and join Eden's rally at the Bull Ring, she's already disrupted Tommy's business affairs once before. Despite this, he shows no interest in discussion. Without further word, Jessie leaves the boardroom and blows her whistle to call a strike.

As the workers down tools, it's evident to Tommy Shelby that Jessie Eden is a woman he cannot ignore.

Like many characters in the Peaky Blinders story, she's also based on a real-life figure from the era. Her life and times may not be as familiar to us as that of Winston Churchill, but as an advocate for women's rights in the workplace, Jessie Eden stood up for her convictions with equal passion.

The real Jessie Eden was born as Jessie Shrimpton in 1902 in Birmingham's Winson Green. Her strong beliefs in women's and worker's rights might well have been formed when her mother served in a munition's factory during the First World War. As a young woman, Jessie found employment at the Joseph Lucas Motor Factory. There, her growing convictions soon earned her the position of shop steward for the Transport and General Workers Union. A brief marriage to Albert Eden in 1923 ended in divorce. Despite being widely believed to have been caused, at least in part, by their conflicting social and political views, Jessie kept his surname.

At the time, workers in Britain were increasingly aware that Russia was undergoing a social and political revolution. The Bolsheviks had risen up to overthrow the government and impose a one-party communist state. With ideals in the air surrounding common ownership of the means of production, and the abolition of class structure, unions in Britain felt empowered in their relationship with government and employers. In 1926, as part of the General Strike, Jessie Eden embraced the mood by calling out the union members in her section at the Lucas plant. This was a brave and notable achievement for a lone female shop steward, not least because the majority of women at the plant were non-unionised and remained in their posts. It was, however, just the first battle cry from the fiery young working-class activist. Joining the British Communist Party only hardened her resolve as a union player. In 1931, in a dispute with management at the Lucas plant, who were seeking to link pay to productivity, Eden would go on to lead ten thousand female workers out of the factory for an entire week.

Jessie Eden's efforts in amassing such support were recognised on both sides as significant. Not only did they further the movement for the unionisation of women workers; ultimately, they led to the owners of the plant rowing back on their proposal. While Eden was acknowledged to be a reliable and efficient worker, with considerable influence among the workforce, she was also seen as a radical who risked further undermining their control. Despite the fact that the plant workers felt they had been pushed to the extreme in terms of pay and performance, cutbacks were imposed by management. The resulting job losses included Jessie's position on the production line.

Jessie Eden's story then moves to Moscow, where she spent several years, having struggled to find employment in Birmingham due to her reputation as both a communist and a union firebrand. There, she is believed to have been involved in supporting women workers before returning to Britain in the late 1930s. Back in Birmingham, where her fierce principles and beliefs had been forged, Eden worked tirelessly in the field of tenants' rights and even stood as a prospective MP for the British Communist Party in the 1945 General Election. She died in 1986 aged eighty-four.

Jessie Eden's professional and romantic involvement with Tommy Shelby in *Peaky Blinders* may be a play on history, but there's no doubt that the woman her character is based upon shared the same ability to turn a spark into a fire for all the right reasons.

THE EDEN CLUB

'This place is under new management, by order of the Peaky Blinders.'

When the Shelby brothers first visit Charles 'Darby' Sabini's Eden Club in London, they walk in quite literally as if they own the joint. Inside, before entering the main space, Tommy, Arthur and John stride through a corridor that's host to wild, hedonistic scenes. The dancefloor is packed with revellers celebrating the sounds of the new Jazz Age, although this party comes to an abrupt end, of course, when the Peaky Blinders make their presence known. Then there's the return, mob-handed, and a takeover bid like no other.

Just as Charles 'Darby' Sabini's character is based on the real-life London gangster, so this particular haunt has roots in reality. In the 1920s, The Eden Social Club formed part of Sabini's underworld empire. It's just that it lacked the space and glamour we see on the screen. Located in a back street near what is now Euston Station, the club in fact occupied a mere two rooms above a garage. It was here in this cramped, dingy space that a disagreement broke out in 1924 that ended with the death of a bookie's runner, the grievous wounding of a doorman and three years' jail time for the perpetrator, Jewish gangster, Alf Solomon.

EMBROIDERY

'I thought it would be worse.'

The Shelbys' Small Heath family home offers a snap-shot into an age the Peaky Blinders are set to leave behind. The furnishings, and even the framed inscription on the wall, are examples of the Edwardian and Victorian taste and flair for embroidery.

From cushions to trims, curtains and armchairs, when Polly holds court from the kitchen table, cigarette in hand, she is surrounded by hand-stitched patterned fabrics that were commonplace in homes across the country at the turn of the twentieth century. When Michael returns to her life, such simple touches help him to feel at ease.

Embroidery has been a popular feature of British life for hundreds of years, with distinctive styles marking different periods. From the eighteenth century onwards, learning to stitch was often considered to be a rite of passage for young women. With little cost involved beyond a needle and thread, embroidery was accessible to all. It's a folk art that was also practised by skilled craft workers, with a place in both palaces and poor houses. The Shelbys might be careering into the Roaring Twenties, a decade of decadence that left the old world behind, but when they gather for family meetings back at Watery Lane, the embroidered furnishings remind them of their roots.

THE EPSOM DERBY

'We'll be drinking with the bloody king!'

It's the greatest event of the year in the horse-racing calendar, as John reminds Polly, and a date with destiny for Tommy Shelby. Here at this prestigious course, with the head of state in attendance, he must outwit Charles 'Darby' Sabini's mob, undertake an audacious mission for the British Intelligence Services and escape with his life.

The Epsom Derby takes place at the Epsom Downs Racecourse in Surrey. Traditionally held in the first week of June – on a Wednesday in the 1920s – this flat race has been an early summer sporting highlight for more than two centuries. In the year that Chief Inspector Campbell would meet his match in Polly Gray, huge crowds flocked to the course from London. While the race itself was the main attraction, a carnival atmosphere prevailed among the spectators, with drinking, betting and sideshows taking place throughout the day.

FABERGÉ EGG

'My jeweller here, he advises me to insist on the Fabergé.'

As Tommy Shelby watches with interest, Alfie Solomons trawls the strongroom containing the treasured jewels that belong to Princess Tatiana Petrovna and her family of aristocratic Russian exiles. He's helping Tommy to pick out his reward in return for helping the Russians steal tanks to support the anti-Bolshevik cause. Sure enough, Alfie's trained eye is quick to identify the sapphires and diamonds among the fakes. It's not enough, however, which is when Tatiana and her uncle and aunt are persuaded by Tommy to bring out the prize in their collection, smuggled from Crimea by Tatiana herself: a glittering Fabergé egg.

Around 1885, a Russian jewellery maker from St Petersburg began to produce a limited number of individual, elaborately jewelled eggs. Each one contained a miniature surprise, such as a golden egg or ruby pendant. Crafted under the supervision of the firm's founder, Gustave Fabergé, these intricate, exquisitely crafted pieces are still regarded as the most celebrated items of jewellery ever made.

The House of Fabergé is believed to have created almost seventy eggs in total. Over the years, a substantial number were presented to tsars Nicholas II and Alexander II as Easter gifts. Following the Russian Revolution of 1917, and the execution or exile of the Imperial royal family, many of the eggs were simply spirited away. While a number are now in private and public collections, and each worth millions, an air of mystery and intrigue regarding the whereabouts and fate of others has only added to their value over time.

The egg reluctantly offered to Alfie Solomons for his appraisal takes his breath away. The Lilies of the Valley was crafted in 1898 and presented to Tsar Nicholas II. It's supported by four cabriolet feet and embellished with lilies on gold stems, diamonds and pearls. The surprise, which rises out of the egg with a twist of a pearl button, takes the form of three miniature portraits of the Tsar and his two daughters, Olga and Tatiana. In *Peaky Blinders*, Father Hughes had hoped to steal the egg from Tommy to present to the wife of an Odd Fellows colleague. In reality, the Lilies of the Valley egg was acquired in 2004 by the House of Fabergé Museum in St Petersburg.

FASCISM

'There are certain species of weeds that no matter how much you tug at them or poison them, they continue to grow back.'

When Winston Churchill offers words of warning about a growing political mood in the country, Tommy Shelby is one step ahead. He knows Sir Oswald Mosley has fascist designs, which is why he invites the soon-to-be-party leader to a ballet performance at his home for Lizzie Shelby's birthday. There, Mosley announces his intent. While the rest of the Shelbys and Aberama Gold are quietly disturbed by his anti-Semitic reasons for the country's economic uncertainty, Tommy listens impassively with plans up his sleeve. Many guests, however, respond enthusiastically to this character, based on a true-life figure who attempted to seize control of the British establishment and impose a fascist regime.

Fascism is a political belief system that places total authority in the hands of one ruler. A fascist maintains that for a country to play to its strengths it requires organising from the top down, with no room for opposing voices. Enemies of the state don't just stop at those who denounce fascism, however, but also include various ethnic groups, who serve as scapegoats for social and economic problems. With its commitment to rebirthing as a nation, and a concept of identity based on country over individual, fascism can be considered to be an extreme form of nationalism.

As a political force, fascism arguably has roots in ancient Rome, when leaders such as Caesar and Augustus called all the shots. It surfaced again in the late 1800s, and attracted popular support following the First World War. Leading fascist believers looked at the way that countries had mobilised for conflict, and considered how this could become a driving force in transforming a nation's fortunes at home and on the world stage. Under Benito Mussolini's rule, Italy by the late 1920s had become an openly fascist nation. In Britain, Oswald Mosley hoped to tap into the same disquiet that had led to Mussolini's success. In 1932, having represented both the Conservative and Labour parties, as well as sitting as an independent MP and attempting to start his own party, Mosley formed the British Union of Fascists.

An effective but controversial orator, Mosley tapped into nationalistic, populist and racist anxieties. As a result, party meetings were frequently met with protests by socialist and Jewish interest groups. It's believed that Mosley enlisted the help of the Billy Boys to serve as security at his rallies, which informs the climatic scenes in season five of *Peaky Blinders* as Tommy plots to take out the party leader and effectively kill off the rise of fascism in the UK.

In reality, for all Mosley's efforts to build a British fascist movement, wider events put an end to his ambitions. With the outbreak of the Second World War, the party was banned and its leader interred. By 1945, with Nazi Germany defeated and Mussolini shot by partisans, fascism in the UK had lost all popular support.

FEDORA

'Take off the hat ...'

In 1924, as Tommy continues to expand Shelby Company Limited's business interests, we see a significant change in the Peaky Blinders' customary dress. As the family gather outside the Shelby Institute for Orphaned Children, the baker boy cap has taken a back seat. Instead, the Shelby brothers and young Michael sport hats that reflect both an Americanisation and sophistication in men's fashion. One year later, Luca Changretta stands before the customs inspector at Liverpool Docks in the same style of headwear, but with murder in mind.

As distinctive as it is classic, the fedora has a sharp, creased crown, a pinched front on each side and a full, soft brim. Often made from felt, the generous brim-width allowed it to be shaped to suit the wearer's taste, which was a novel feature at the time. Sure enough, Tommy wears his fedora with the front curved down and one side lifted, in keeping with his swagger.

In America, having started out as a hat style for women in the late 1880s, the fedora crept into men's fashion in the late nineteenth century before taking centre stage in the 1920s. Alongside the Homburg – another Peaky Blinders' choice – men tended to choose earthy colours that matched their suits, or with a contrasting band around the body of the hat. While the fedora hat came to represent the Prohibition era, with no self-respecting gangster seen without one, it also gained some prestige when adopted as the hat of choice by Edward, Prince of Wales, who would fleetingly become king in 1936 before abdicating in the same year. As for *Peaky Blinders*, there's no doubt that when Michael Gray returns from America with his new bride, Gina, his fedora signifies that he's a changed man on several levels.

THE FIRST WORLD WAR

'Mr Churchill, you should know that I am a former British soldier and if you look at my war record you will see I fought bravely . . .'

Peaky Blinders opens in 1919, shortly after the Allied troops returned home from the frontline, and yet the First World War looms large over the story of Tommy Shelby's subsequent rise to power. Even in his letter to the Secretary of State, setting out the terms for his involvement in carrying out an assassination for the crown, Tommy writes as one veteran to another. The war affected all aspects of life, and society now attempts to recover from one of the most significant events in world history.

In the years before the war, which broke out in 1914, tensions were running high across Europe. Fears of political instability, military build-ups and the rise of nationalism had led to many countries forming alliances. Some were forged on a public platform. Others were struck in secret. Arguably, this gave rise to a situation in which an isolated international incident could spark a global conflict.

In 1914, Archduke Franz Ferdinand – an heir to the Austro-Hungarian throne – was assassinated by nationalists in Sarajevo. The Austrian government held Serbia accountable, threatening to invade, only for Russia to step in as Serbian allies. Within a matter of weeks, the situation had escalated to draw in major powers. Germany stepped up to back the Austro-Hungarians – the two becoming the principal players in the Central Powers along with Bulgaria and the Ottoman Empire – by declaring war on Russia. Crucially, the Germans also struck out at France before they could support their own pact with Russia, and invaded Belgium at the same time in a bid for dominance. At this point, aligned with both Russia and France – and known as the Allied Powers – Britain and her Empire territories honoured their pact by declaring war on the Central Powers.

At the outbreak of hostilities, the British Army was made up of volunteers. With under half a million troops, it was also relatively small compared to

German numbers. This changed between 1914 and 1915 when Lord Kitchener, the Secretary of State for War, urged young men to sign up and fight in the name of King George V. It's likely that Tommy Shelby and his brothers answered this call before conscription was introduced in 1916 and military service became compulsory.

Fighting the conflict on two fronts – facing Russia to the east while pushing towards France through Belgium – the Germans pursued an aggressive military strategy. In September 1914, British troops met the German army to the north-east of Paris. While the Allies succeeded in preventing the Central Powers from advancing further, both sides duly dug in. The Western Front, as it was known by troops for the next three years, was a line defined by many brutal incursions and battles including the Somme and Verdun. Under relentless shelling, soldiers on both sides suffered terrible hardship and loss.

Meanwhile from 1914 to 1916 on the Eastern Front, the Germans had held the Allied Powers at bay. Disillusionment set in among the Russian troops, compounded by impoverished conditions back home and resentment towards the ruling classes. When this culminated in the 1917 Bolshevik Revolution, Russia negotiated an armistice with the Central Powers and effectively ended its role in the war.

That same year, provoked by German attacks on merchant ships, America joined the conflict. By now, both sides had suffered greatly fighting on land, in the air and at sea. The Allied Powers had failed to gain the upper hand by taking the fight to Turkey and the Ottoman Empire, while the Central Powers were feeling the economic effects of waging a war on a global scale. With troops from the USA bolstering numbers in France, the Allies were able to begin pushing the Germans into retreat. Towards the end of 1918, the Central Powers started to crack. With defeats on the battlefront, and anti-war protests at home, Germany was forced to concede.

By the end of hostilities, 3.8 million British troops had served their country in a war that saw 886,000 fail to return and countless more injured. A huge demobilisation effort followed that lasted into 1919. It meant that when Tommy Shelby first rode out through the streets of Small Heath, privately suffering from nightmares about his wartime experience on the Western Front, he would not have been out of uniform for long.

FLAPPER

'It's a party ... and I'm going to enjoy myself.'

The grand reopening of the Garrison, following the IRA bombing in 1921, opens the doors on an era in *Peaky Blinders* in which women like Polly celebrated their newfound independence and freedom. In many ways, the flapper personified the concept of the Roaring Twenties, in which Europe and America recovered from the First World War both economically and culturally, gaining a newfound confidence. Increased transatlantic travel and communication enabled the exchange of everything from liberal ideas to style movements and a general sense that horizons were expanding. After years of smoke and darkness, the sparkle of glamour and the chance to break from conformity proved irresistible to a generation of young women.

In *Peaky Blinders*, Lizzie Stark is the first to dress up in the fashion that swept across from America in the early 1920s. She's at the bar on the reopening night wearing a short chiffon dress, beads and a headpiece, smoking a cigarette in a long holder with a cocktail on the go. For Lizzie, it might just be for this special occasion, but soon the flapper scene spreads its wings across the decade. From the hedonistic scenes at Charles 'Darby' Sabini's Eden Club to Princess Tatiana Petrovna's sequinned twinkle and Gatsby glamour, it's an iconic style that captures the sense of liberty and spirit of the age.

FORTUNE-TELLING

'Read my leaves, Pol. You haven't done my leaves in ages.'

Polly Gray is a spiritual woman, but not just in the conventional religious sense. While she attends mass and confession, her beliefs also embrace the psychic realm.

Troubled by recurring dreams about her long-lost daughter, Polly visits a Gypsy medium. Her faith in fortune-telling is undeterred when she learns the old woman has simply told her what she wanted to hear about the little girl. In fact, she goes on to reveal her own gift when she reads the tea leaves for Lizzie to help determine her romantic destiny.

Fortune-telling is closely linked to Romani culture. With strong spiritual beliefs entwined into the way of life, it's accepted within communities that some members – always female and known as 'drabardi' – have the ability to foretell the future or commune with a higher realm.

Reading palms and tarot cards have been popular forms of Gypsy fortune-telling for centuries, as has the ability to divine the future from reading coffee grounds or tea leaves. When Polly peers into Lizzie's cup at the patterns formed by the dregs on the inside, she tells her with absolute certainty that she's expecting a baby. It's not a fanciful form of entertainment for either woman. In fact, Lizzie gives up whiskey on Polly's advice and sticks to stout instead.

How to read tea leaves

- The art of divining fortunes from tea or coffee sediment is known as tasseography.
- After drinking the tea, the fortune-teller asks the client to swirl the dregs and hand over the cup.
- Holding the cup handle in the dominant hand, the fortune-teller slowly turns the cup and reads from the rim downwards. Broadly speaking, the top of the cup represents the present with the far future at the bottom and base.
- Drawing on imagination and intuition, and sometimes by referring to charts that they may regard as significant, practitioners look for symbols in the dregs. A heart shape might represent love, for example, or an anchor denote stability.
- Some fortune-tellers use a forecasting cup, which divides the inside into a grid containing visual cues to assist in interpretation.

- Customs of the ritual differ from one fortune-teller to another. If you're tempted to try your hand, it's about opening your mind's eye as you peer into the cup with the same confidence and self-belief as a Peaky Blinder matriarch who's been entrusted to divine the future.

THE GARRISON TAVERN

'Men always tell their troubles to a barmaid.'

As a location, it sits at the heart of *Peaky Blinders*. As Grace says herself, it's a confessional of sorts. At the same time, the Garrison Tavern undergoes a very subtle and important interior transformation to reflect the changing world outside.

Our introduction to the pub on the corner of Garrison Lane and Watery Lane takes place in 1919. Here, when Tommy first walks through the double doors, a hush descends among the drinkers at the bar. With spittoons at their feet, sawdust on the floorboards and the air thick with smoke, we could be in a saloon bar in the Wild West. Instead, this working man's pub in industrial Birmingham at the turn of the century provides respite from the grind of a hard, austere life.

Two years later, having been blown up by the IRA, the Garrison Tavern is rebuilt to reflect the rising fortunes of Shelby Company Ltd. Gifted to Arthur by Tommy, the pub becomes a place of song and celebration, with window drapes, a gently curving bar, softer lighting and a music hall atmosphere. The deal brokering continues in the Peaky Blinders' unofficial boardroom – the corner snug – but like any drinking establishment in a country getting back on its feet after the war, it's a place for both business and pleasure.

By 1929, following the stock market crash, the pub has been stripped of its fabrics and furnishings. In a sense, it's returned to its true purpose as a simple place to escape from the pressures of life. What's striking about the pub ten years on is the addition of stained-glass windows. Now, the light that cuts through the gloom could be illuminating a cathedral. For the patrons who drink here, and who – when he walks in – thank Tommy Shelby MP for his efforts to transform their lives, there's no doubt the Garrison Tavern has become a place that offers solace, hope and redemption.

Interior essentials: classic Garrison furnishings for the Peaky Blinder pub

TABLES AND CHAIRS

Oak furniture was commonplace in the 1920s. The Garrison's early incarnation was largely furnished by circular wooden tables and simple spindle-back chairs, with no cushioning and rounded backrests. Upholstered banquette seating and rectangular tables can be found in the booths, providing a little more comfort and some discretion thanks to the wood-panelled dividing screens.

SPITTOONS

When Grace is at her job interview for the position of barmaid, the receptacles she collects to empty certainly look handsome. The unpleasant fact is, though, that they're largely full of black spit from tobacco-chewing or pipe-smoking patrons. The spittoon, or cuspidor, was a regular feature in British pubs from the late nineteenth century until they fell out of favour in the late 1920s and early 30s on hygiene grounds, not to mention the introduction of carpeted floors.

The Garrison Tavern spittoons are made from brass with flat bottoms to minimise the risk of tipping over if kicked by accident. Bar staff also used them to pour away the dregs from glasses when clearing tables, which added to the volume of 'tobacco juice' that Grace shows no disgust in handling as she demonstrates her suitability for the post.

ASHTRAYS
With spitting covered by the spittoon, the Garrison patrons can rely on thick, heavy glass receptacles to tamp their cigarettes and crush the stubs. At the same time, there is an element of style and design to the pub's ashtrays; a feature that reflects the growing number of female smokers in the early twentieth century.

LAMPS AND CHANDELIERS
In Britain, electricity only took over from gas, oil-lamp and candle as the main source of lighting during the First World War. By 1919, with the fabric lampshade in its infancy, the harsh glare from an electric bulb was often softened by opaque glass domes. The wall-mounted lamps inside the Garrison are a classic example. They provide a warm perimeter light and leave the candelabra chandeliers to provide the main illumination. With upturned bulbs instead of candles on the end of each arm, they represent a significant moment in lighting evolution.

In the refurbished Garrison, two years later, the lighting has acquired sophistication, a little colour and some foreshadowing of the future for the Shelby family business. As Tommy walks among the revellers at the grand opening, there's no escaping the fact that the wall-mounted lights are now capped by blood-red lampshades.

GARROTTE

'My brother is dead ...'

Simple to hide but deadly effective, the garrotte is the assassin's weapon of choice in several key *Peaky Blinders* scenes. Essentially a ligature used for strangulation, it's deployed with an element of surprise on one unsuspecting man as he stands in the shadows of a children's puppet theatre show. Sneaking up from behind, the IRA killer snaps the garrotte around his victim's throat, killing him with the minimum of noise. Later, Arthur Shelby threatens to go the same way when ambushed in the boxing hall dressing rooms by Changretta's men. It's an attempt on his life that Tommy turns to his advantage by announcing his death from the ring to fool Luca and his mob.

In America through the 1930s, the garotte was often used in Mafia-related killings. As well as being the assassin's tool of choice, a more elaborate but equally brutal version was used for capital punishment in Spain until the mid 1970s.

THE 1926 GENERAL STRIKE

'People are not afraid any more.'

When union leader Jessie Eden meets Tommy Shelby in the factory boardroom to discuss workers' pay and conditions, her boldness reflects the mood of the times.

In 1925, when the exchange takes place, the UK's mining industry was struggling. High demand for coal during the First World War had compromised reserves. At the same time, faced with stiff competition from overseas, mine owners were cutting pay while increasing workers' hours. This led to rising dissatisfaction and resentment among miners, and also a sense of solidarity across trade unions.

Within a year, despite attempted interventions from Stanley Baldwin's government, relations between the workforce and mine owners had completely broken down. On 3 May 1926, the TUC (Trades Union Congress) announced a general strike in support of the miners that saw over one and a half million workers walk out. The strength of support for the strike came as a surprise to the government and business owners, many of whom saw their operations come to a standstill. At the same time, as the walk-out stretched beyond a week, strikers who were already on the breadline and concerned about their jobs began to waver.

As well as some weakening in resolve, a point of contractual law persuaded the TUC to call off the strike. Ultimately, union leaders were forced to recognise that only the miners were entitled to down tools in their dispute with their employers. By inciting wider members to come out in solidarity, the TUC had left themselves liable for breaching contracts of employment. The 1926 General Strike ended on 12 May, although the miners held out until the autumn before admitting defeat. What started as a reflection of rising discontent across the country's workforce – and an unarguably impressive show of strength – ended with little sense of achievement or victory for the unions or the miners at the heart of the dispute.

GIN

'I will pour you some gin, that I make myself, from my father's recipe. Distilled for the eradication of seemingly incurable sadness.'

Gin drinking in Britain has a lively heritage, having first taken off in the seventeenth century following tax cuts on production. Becoming cheaper to buy than a beer, and simple to make with basic equipment, it became established as a wildly popular drink as well as creating serious social problems. Licensing measures brought the situation under some control, and yet behind closed doors the amateur gin-maker continued to serve the black market into the early twentieth century.

Created from a family recipe, Tommy Shelby's gin is infused with personal passion. It's a solo sideline to the family's business empire, which he oversees with the care and attention of a true craftsman. The basic distillation process involves heating a base spirit such as vodka with aromatic botanicals. This is done in a still

– an apparatus that allows the vapour to rise, cool and then run off for collection.

Distilling gin allows maximum extraction of flavour and essential oils from the botanicals. It also results in a more concentrated spirit, and today, in the UK and many other countries, a licence is required to produce gin using this method.

Steeping gin requires no such paperwork; it merely demands a little patience and creativity. In this legal method, the botanicals are simply added to the base spirit and then left so that the flavours infuse over time. Here's what you need to make the most of your back room or basement.

Steeping your own gin

EQUIPMENT
- A sterilised glass jar with lid or clip top × 2
- A stirring spoon
- A sieve

INGREDIENTS
Vodka is the most common base spirit when it comes to making gin at home. A decent bottle will produce the best results. You'll also need to create a botanical mix. This is a blend of natural aromatic ingredients – led by juniper berries – that helps to impart the distinctive gin taste. Start with this basic, traditional recipe and then get creative with flavour:

- 30 grams juniper berries (lightly crushed with the back of the spoon if fresh, but dried is fine)
- Two cardamom pods

- 10 grams coriander seeds
- Half a cinnamon stick
- A small piece of lemon peel
- A small piece of orange peel

METHOD
1. Add the botanical mix to the jar and then pour in the vodka.
2. Stir, and then seal the jar.
3. Store in a cool, dry place for two days.
4. Remove the botanicals by pouring the contents through a sieve into the other jar.
5. Seal the jar and leave for another two days.
6. Your steeped gin is now ready to enjoy.

GLASSES

'I know a man who can make you a pair of these ... he's a magician, mate. A magician. So, not only will you be able to read your newspaper, but you'll also be able to see into the future.'

Alfie Solomons' recommendation follows Tommy's admission that his cracked skull – at the hands of Father Murphy's men – has compromised his eyesight. In the 1920s, glasses were available on prescription, with lenses fixed within predominantly oval frames for both men and women.

Having recovered from his injuries, Tommy increasingly relies on spectacles for clarity, whether reading or writing at his desk or giving a speech in the House of Commons. He has several pairs in the same rounded shape, with arms that finish in a pronounced curl. At the time, glasses that fitted around the ears in this way were considered ground-breaking. Up until the early years of the twentieth century, the armless pince-nez was the dominant eyepiece – like the pair Alfie wears on a chain around his neck – which was fixed in place by squeezing the bridge of the frame across the nose.

As the 1920s progressed, different styles of glasses emerged along with the concept of eyewear that protected against the glare of the sun. Polly Gray is an early adopter of sunglasses, which would go on to become a mainstream fashion item in the 1930s.

GOOSE

'There will be twenty-seven guests for Christmas dinner tomorrow . . . I asked Johnny Dogs if he knew anyone who liked to eat goose, and he said he knew twenty-six.'

Historically, turkey is relatively new as the main dish on 25 December. Up until the Victorian era, the dark meat and full-bodied flavour of a roast goose was the festive choice in households that could afford such luxury. Through the nineteenth century and into the next, after turkey became the popular and more afford-able choice, goose was still considered to be the choice cut for the Christmas connoisseur. For a figure rising through the social ranks, it's a natural choice for a man like Tommy Shelby.

In 1925, as Tommy prepares to celebrate the season at Arrow House with his son, Charlie, he asks his housekeeper, Mary, to make sure that the new chef prepares ten birds for his guests. It's a request that ends in butchery and bloodshed in the kitchen that goes far beyond the catering plan. After Tommy has dispatched a would-be killer in his midst and sent the treacherous chef back to Mr Sabini with a message, events somewhat overtake the festive celebrations. Had Christmas dinner been served as planned, however, guests could have expected a roasted goose that many still regard as superior to the turkey.

GRACE SHELBY INSTITUTE FOR ORPHANED CHILDREN

'I didn't come here to make a speech, but I will say this. These children are now safe.'

To honour the memory of his wife, following her death by an assassin's bullet meant for him, Tommy Shelby opens an orphanage in her name. It's the last thing Grace had been working on, and a reflection of the growing unease at the turn of the twentieth century about the welfare of vulnerable young people.

In Victorian times, children without parents or a family member willing to take responsibility for them – or who had simply been abandoned – were said to be unfortunate rather than deserving of the right to care and protection. Orphanages existed to care for babies and very young children who could not fend for themselves, but were often full to capacity. As a result, older children often ended up in the workhouse or fending for themselves on the streets.

Public concern for abandoned or orphaned children rose steeply in the mid-1800s. Private benefactors and organisations began to establish orphanages, often with involvement from the Church, while the establishment of Ragged Schools for impoverished children in London inspired similar movements across the country. By the late 1800s, the orphanage movement had expanded to cater not just for babies but also for children suffering from hardship or neglect.

As a system of care, orphanages and schools for the poor in the early decades of the 1900s left boys and girls vulnerable to cruelty and abuse. Later, Father Hughes, seeks a footing in the running of the Shelby orphanage, it becomes clear that such institutions could become a source of danger as much as protection for vulnerable children. It's also something Tommy and Polly are forced to deal with on hearing testimonies from children at a convent school funded by the Grace Shelby Institute. They pay a visit to the Mother Superior. Face to face with the Peaky Blinders, she is unrepentant over her conduct, including allegations that a child in her care has taken her own life, but silenced when Tommy withdraws further funding and vows to take the children into their own institution. Just to reinforce their position, Polly leaves the Mother Superior in no doubt that her safety is now in danger as a consequence.

By the middle of the twentieth century, an increase in state intervention in child welfare and the evolution of the care system spelt an end to the orphanage era.

GYPSY

'I can charm a dog. Gypsy witchcraft. And those I can't I kill with my bare hands.'

The Shelbys are proud of their heritage. It lies at the heart of their identity. At times, such as when he's facing a canine threat at the hands of Father Hughes, Tommy uses people's preconceptions of the Gypsy way of life to undermine their understanding of what makes him tick. Even as the Shelbys make their mark on modern life between the wars, the ancient customs and conventions of their forebears inform all aspects of their lives.

In *Peaky Blinders*, Tommy and his brothers – along with Aunt Polly Gray and her son, Michael – are primarily from Irish Traveller descent. This indigenous ethnic group is sometimes associated with Romani people, who began to arrive in Europe from the north Indian subcontinent around the tenth century. Both Irish Travellers and the Romani are nomadic communities. Historically known as Gypsies – which is considered to be a culturally sensitive term today – their way of life was often met with prejudice and marginalisation. The sense of identity for both Irish Travellers and Romani came from the importance of freedom in living on the move rather than through ties to a homeland. With no connection to place, however, such groups through the centuries were regarded as outsiders by settled communities and treated with distrust and even outright hostility.

Since each roaming community relied on strong oral traditions to preserve its history and way of life, the link between Irish Travellers and the Romani people is not comprehensively documented. There are similarities – in *Peaky Blinders* a wedding takes place between members of the two groups – as well as much that sets them apart. Both, for example, have their own languages – Romani and the Irish Traveller's tongue, Shelta – but linguistically these are very different from each other. With links to both cultures, by birthright and marriage, the Shelbys and the Grays reflect this middle ground. Indeed, when the Shelbys face prejudice they are referred to as 'didicoys', which is a term sometimes used to describe a Traveller who does not just have Romani parentage.

In the mid-nineteenth century, famine and poverty in Ireland forced many people to start new lives in England, Wales and Scotland. Irish Travellers were among this exodus, which is how Tommy, Arthur, Ada, John, Finn and Michael effectively became a settled generation living in Birmingham. While they lead essentially conventional lives by comparison to their Gypsy forebears, their roots are never far from the surface.

Catholicism is central to many Irish Travellers, as embodied by Polly Gray, who attends both mass and confession at church. The spirit world and superstitions also play a role in Gypsy life, especially the Romani people. In the early twentieth century, fortune-telling using anything from tea leaves to tarot cards and crystal balls was said to be a fruitful source of income for Gypsy seers when offering their services to the outside world. In fact, the biggest link between the travelling and settled communities was economic. Gypsies took on seasonal farming work, traded horses, mended household utensils and practised crafts like making and mending tools. Their skills were rich and diverse, particularly when it came to living off the land as they travelled through the countryside. The central issue faced by both the Romani people and Irish Travellers was in securing work from a wider world that was so deeply wary of them.

In the early 1900s, Gypsy life was governed by clear codes of ethics and conduct. As closed communities, often comprising a small number of extended families, they endeavoured to maintain their sense of social order with rules on morality and cleanliness, gender roles and social ranking. While men served as the head of the family, women formed the heart, and tended to earn respect through motherhood and age. Gypsy elders were even considered in royal terms. Polly Gray makes no secret of the fact that her grandmother, Birdie Boswell, was a Gypsy princess who married a Shelby, while Tommy pays a visit to the Lee family matriarch, Zilpha Lee, who quite literally holds court in her covered wagon. There, Tommy arranges the marriage between his brother, John, and 'a girl in the Lee family who's gone a bit wild', to settle a dispute between the two clans. The Gypsy wedding that takes place in front of the wagons between John and Esme, conducted by Johnny Dogs, includes a Romani tradition of cutting the palm of both bride and groom and then mingling the blood 'so two families become one family'.

Today, the Irish Traveller community in the UK, along with the Romani people (now sometimes referred to as English Travellers), continue to battle against marginalisation and stereotyping while protecting their way of life. The 2011 census of England and Wales recorded 58,000 residents identifying as Gypsy or Traveller, which amounted to just 0.1 per cent of the resident population.

HAIRSTYLES

'Tommy, when a pikey walks in with hair like that, you got to ask yourself, "Have I made a mistake?"'

In a story as visually striking as *Peaky Blinders*, the Shelby brothers' haircuts stand head and shoulders above all else.

Despite Alfie Solomons' provocative view, history largely informed the distinctive look for Tommy, Arthur, John and Finn in particular. From 1910, through the First World War and up to the 1940s, working-class men wore their hair close to the scalp at the back and sides. The top was left longer and often swept or combed to one side. The undercut, as it became known, requires little or no grading between the short and longer lengths. This style is believed to have originated in the early twentieth century when most men had their hair cut at home by family members with no training. Shorter hair was known to reduce the risk of lice, and it didn't get in the way during a fight – as recognised by street gangs in Glasgow at the time, as well as in the Midlands.

The undercut endured through the First World War for the sake of smartness and practicality, arguably becoming more pronounced through the use of military clippers for the back and sides. Laura 'Loz' Schiavo – the hair and make-up designer for the first season of *Peaky Blinders* – drew inspiration for styles from vintage photographs featured in a book about criminals in 1920s Sydney, Australia, called *Crooks Like Us*, by Peter Doyle. The resulting look for the Shelby brothers is both razor-sharp and arresting. Sporting variations of the same undercut, they would go on to influence contemporary men's fashion when the show first aired in 2013.

Tommy Shelby

In the early years of his ascendency, the head of the Shelby Company Limited wears his hair high, but tight to the scalp at the back and sides. The top is then cut in textures and left slightly longer at the front to make the most of a natural wave. It's a harsh, uncompromising look in keeping with his character. Later, as his business dealings demand an air of respectability, so the back and sides are clipped to grade three in length to soften the contrast with the top.

Arthur Shelby

Another classic undercut, but with the contrast between short and long set to extreme. Unlike his brother, Tommy, Arthur wears his hear swept back at the top. It's also a little longer, and more likely to fall out of place in the wake of a fist fight. When Arthur briefly tries out a life of domestication in the countryside with his wife, Linda, he allows the usually close-cropped sides to grow out with the top, creating a romantic, almost Byronic look. It doesn't last long, however. Back to business, it's a buzz-cut to the scalp at the back and sides, and clawed back on top with fingers that are primed to close into fists.

John Shelby

A blend of his two older brothers' look in style, John's undercut has the same severity as Arthur's at the back

and sides but with Tommy's shape and texture up top.
It's much shorter, however, with little styling required.
This is a no-nonsense, minimal-care crop that can be
combed into a smart, sharp look or be left simply to
take care of itself.

Finn Shelby

Finn's strong cheekbones bring out the best in his
undercut, which is shaved to the scalp at the back and
side and then worked up on top. It's not quite a quiff or
a pompadour, but is a look worn with pride that
commands respect and attention. As he matures, Finn
begins to echo older brother, Arthur, by sweeping back
the top.

Michael Gray

A no-nonsense cut for Polly's long-lost son neatly
reflects his attitude and outlook. Foregoing the undercut, Michael Gray opts for a sharp, short back and
sides. It's clean, trim and tapered, and works well with
his wavy hair.

STAY SHARP

Both the undercut and short back and sides are
intended to be smart, workmanlike hairstyles requiring little fuss through the day. In the early twentieth
century, many men used pomade to style their hair and
keep it in place. A male grooming product made from
beeswax or petroleum, this oily substance gave the hair
a heavy, wet, shining look that clung to the scalp. It also

allowed men to quickly and confidently comb their hair into shape, and became a popular accessory for more than thirty years. In *Peaky Blinders*, everyone from Freddie Thorne and Bonnie Gold to Billy Kimber, Father Hughes and Sir Oswald Mosley share the same reliance on pomade to maintain their appearance.

Over time, stiffening agents were introduced into pomades that allowed for more creativity and ambition, such as the 1950s quiff, and used substitutes for oil that allowed it to be washed out more easily. Thirty years earlier, however, as the Shelbys stamp their presence on Small Heath and beyond, this old-school hair product was as vital as the street-gang style that relied on it.

Peaky Blinders isn't a showcase for sharp men's haircuts only. The female characters also showcase iconic styles that celebrate fashion through history. The series' creators take a magpie approach in this respect, picking off iconic looks that aren't always pinned to the precise reality of the age, and yet throwing a light on styles that might otherwise be forgotten altogether.

Polly Gray

As the family matriarch, one who ran the Shelby business during the war, Polly Gray cuts a commanding presence from the outset of *Peaky Blinders*. When she ambushes John as he exits an alley, pressing the muzzle of a gun to his temple, her long, crow-dark ringlets fall from under a broad-brimmed felt hat. Together with her black, layered skirt and blouse shirt, she's a woman in charge with an Edwardian sense of authority.

As the Shelby family head into the 1920s, primed to steal the moment, Polly's changing character is reflected not just by her wardrobe but her hair styling. At the reopening of the Garrison, she lets her hair tumble freely over her shoulders. Combined with a glittering red dress and fur stole, it's a bold, arresting look from a strong woman who knows what she wants.

In keeping with the fashion of the times, Polly goes on to wear her hair in a loose bob. Cut short to the nape of the neck, and with a fringe to frame her face, it's a dramatically different look from previous styles that celebrated the growing independence of women. Considered to be improper and unconventional when it first appeared in the early twentieth century, by the early to mid-1920s the bob haircut had become hugely popular. In particular, it was a look strongly associated with the flapper generation of young women who made a virtue of free thinking and expression.

One year on from her escape from death at the gallows, Polly's sense of purpose and assurance deserts her. Locked away in her townhouse, in the midst of a breakdown and communing with ghosts, she appears to take solace in her Gypsy roots. She has grown her hair long and wild to reflect this, gathered back in a loose band but coming untethered as she drowns her sorrows.

By 1925, back on the Shelby Company Limited payroll, Polly's rebellious streak leads the way. Fired up by the cause of women's rights in the workplace, she cuts a commanding presence on leading her female staff on strike. Her hair, styled in a short, tousled crop, is both elegant and uncompromising. It's a look that she takes a step further by the time Michael returns from America in 1929 with his new wife, Gina. Stepping out of the Wolseley at the train station, respondent in a suit, waistcoat, tie and shades, and with her dark, coiffured hair crowned by a fedora hat, this is Polly Gray as *femme fatale* – the iconic female in early twentieth-century culture from art to opera, and then later in *film noir*, for example featuring Marlene Dietrich, Lauren Bacall and Ava Gardner. From her roots in a pre-war era, and through her ascendency during the 1920s, Polly Gray's hairstyle is a subtle but striking reflection of both the changing world and transformation in her character.

Grace Shelby

When the girl from Galway, and a secret agent of the crown, walks into the Garrison in the hope of finding work behind the bar, landlord Harry Fenton tells her the vacancy has been filled. Buttoned into her green coat and broad-brimmed hat, and with her straw-coloured hair falling over her shoulders in loose twists, Grace Burgess looks completely out of place. It's only when she demonstrates that appearances can be deceptive by emptying the spittoons without complaint that Harry changes his mind and offers her the job.

As Tommy's guest at the races, Grace wears her hair

Grace understands the power of first impressions, and uses this to her advantage. In the first decades of the twentieth century, especially living in the smoke and grime of an industrial heartland like Birmingham, women tended to tie back their hair, wearing it up in a bun or under a hat. Grace allows hers to fall loose like a true country girl in the city, and such a disarming presence earns her a place in Tommy's Shelby's world.

As Tommy's guest at the races, Grace wears her hair

down once more. What's striking about this choice is that all the women at the event have pinned or braided their hair. Without doubt, she's a free spirit who's as proud of her Celtic roots as Tommy is of his Gypsy heritage.

When love conquers all, and she finally joins the Shelby family fold, Grace makes her first nod to the fashion of the times with a chin-length bob set with waves for style and elegance. In the 1920s and 30s, women often created this effect – an alternative to curls – by using a combing technique called the finger wave. A longer-lasting method called marcelling also gained popularity once heated curling irons became available. Both Linda Shelby and Gina Gray employ this style, which helped define the characterful look of this era.

Ada Thorne

The bob cut that frames Ada's face became a fashion mainstay through the 1920s. The short or mid-length style, cut straight around the head with a fringe at the front, was invented by a Polish hairdresser called Antoine de Paris and took shape in select European salons over the course of the preceding decade. For Ada, a young woman seeking to distance herself from the Shelby name, it's a practical and no-nonsense cut that reflects her desire to lead a simple life. Unfortunately for her, even marriage can't sever those family bonds. Following the death of her husband, Freddie, she returns with reluctance to the fold.

A spell in America, expanding Shelby Company Limited, sees Ada come back with both assurance and wealth. Her hair is still styled into a loose bob, but rather than being scraped to one side, her fringe is set with glamorous finger waves. She is an independent woman who has tasted glamour on the other side of the Atlantic, and now turns heads where she would once have gone unnoticed.

Lizzie Stark

As if seeking to escape her early life as a prostitute, Lizzie Stark seizes each opportunity to immerse herself in the changing fashions of the era. After John announces what will be a doomed plan to marry her, and Tommy first checks to see whether she's really given up her old trade, she wears her long hair pinned loosely, like Polly Gray. Life is hard for Lizzie. She does her best with what little she has. There's no glamour in her appearance, but even Tommy can see a strong inner kindness and beauty.

Within a year, at the reopening of the Garrison, Lizzie has cut her hair into a chin-length bob, artfully curled inwards at the ends, and embraced the freedom of the flapper age. It's a look she develops and refines over time, adding volume with waves but always maintaining the sharp lines to complement her strong features. By the time she and Tommy become husband and wife – and like all the principal female characters in *Peaky Blinders* – Lizzie's hair styling has become a measure of her growing poise and confidence.

HATPIN

'I'm not afraid of you.'

For Polly Gray, a hatpin isn't just a decorative means of keeping her headwear in place. In confronting the barmaid and secret agent of the crown, Grace Burgess, about her true purpose, she draws the sharp-pointed, six-inch-long accessory between her fingers should she need to use it as a weapon.

The hatpin first became a fashion feature for women in the early 1800s. Used to hold veils and wimples in place, the pin tip is carefully pushed through the side of the headpiece, under a lock of hair and then back through to fasten it in place. The head of the pin was often ornate, which made it an attractive as well as a practical feature.

The early twentieth century saw a fashion for big, broad-brimmed hats, and the hatpin – frequently in an even longer form – became an ever more essential item in securing these. Strikingly, Polly wasn't alone in considering such an eye-catching accessory to be a useful means of self-defence. With increasing independence, especially following the Suffragette movement, reports grew of women fending off unwanted attention by brandishing the pin from their hat. The practice divided opinion, many women considering the hatpin to be a reassuring means of protecting themselves, but others – mainly men – calling for the pin tips to be covered by law. For Polly Gray, when facing anyone from a suspect agent of the crown to an abusive nun, her hatpin was always on hand to help her get her point across in no uncertain terms.

HIP FLASK

'Drink it. You're going to need it.'

It's always within reach for Tommy, Arthur and co., and serves to instil everything from comfort to courage. Through morning, noon and night, a nip of Irish whiskey from the hip flask is often all it takes for the Shelbys to steel their resolve.

While people have always liked a drink on the move since Roman times, the hip flask hit the heights of popularity as the Peaky Blinders made their name. Often contoured to fit snugly against the body – not just the hip but the breast pocket or, for women, tucked inside a garter – the flask was made from pewter or glass, and later from steel, sometimes encased in leather and filled with a hard drink of choice. The cap was generally attached to the bottle to prevent it from being lost. Hip flasks also came in different sizes, with the standard eight-ounce vessel providing five spirit measures.

During the First World War, many soldiers considered the hip flask to be a vital piece of kit, but it was Prohibition in 1920s America that saw its use become widespread on civvy street. With drinking outlawed in the States, but underground liquor widely available, this discreet little accessory became an ideal means to sneak a shot without drawing attention. In fact, the term 'bootleg' is said to have come from the fact that many drinkers chose to tuck their hip flasks inside their socks. The popularity of the flask in America soon boosted its use in Britain, where it become a perfectly acceptable means for everyone across all classes to enjoy a quiet drink, even if the rules said otherwise. Design and personalisation shaped the hip flask through the interwar years, and to this day it continues to strike a quiet note of rebellion when popped out in public.

HOMBURG

'Who's gonna stop us? Nobody.'

As the Peaky Blinders arrive for the opening of the Grace Shelby Institute for Orphaned Children, it's a surprise to see they have traded in their flat caps for stylish brimmed hats. It's a reflection of the fashion of the mid-1920s, with the familiar fedora proving to a popular choice for men and also women through to the 1950s.

While John and Tommy sport variations of the same style of fedora, with the pinched front and shaped brim, brother Arthur's headwear is subtly different but enough to set him apart. The homburg is distinguishable at the front because it features no pinch or double dent. It has the same creased crown as the fedora, as well as a ribbon band, but with a flatter brim that finishes in an upturned curl. The homburg was popularised by the heir apparent, Edward VII, in the late nineteenth century, and later by two prime ministers: Sir Anthony Eden and, perhaps most famously, Sir Winston Churchill.

For a hat that looks broadly similar to the fedora, the homburg is in fact closely related to its predecessor, the top hat. Originating in the German district that gave the hat its name, the homburg was considered to be a less formal, softer, and more refined, stylish alternative. The design continued to evolve in the early decades of the twentieth century, the hat, over time, becoming more compact and streamlined in response to the growing trend towards wearing the fedora. Both hats subsequently declined in popularity during the 1950s as fashion moved into a more casual style.

HORSE RACING

'Fast women and slow horses will ruin your life.'

As a popular spectator sport, horse racing has a long and noble history in Britain. By 1919, when the Peaky Blinders sought to control the courses, flat race meetings and, increasingly, national hunt racing attracted both huge public interest and considerable sums of money.

Through introduction of rules and regulations from the mid-eighteenth century onwards, the Jockey Club was largely responsible for shaping horse racing into major events. Most significantly, they organised five annual flat race meetings into a series known as the English Classics, which included the jewel in the crown: The Epsom Derby.

By the early 1920s, with licensed gambling restricted to racecourses, and large sums of money exchanged, gangs led by Billy Kimber and Charles 'Darby' Sabini duly moved in to 'protect' the bookmakers in exchange for a cut of the takings. In the power struggle that followed, the two sides frequently came into conflict on race days.

'The Racecourse Wars', as the feud became known in the press, lasted through much of the decade. A truce was called when the gangs agreed to divide control of the courses along geographical lines, with the south going to Sabini's London mob and Kimber taking control of the north. Eventually, following an upswing in efforts by the police, the Jockey Club and the newly formed Bookmakers Protection Association, the gangs were steadily forced to retreat from the racecourses.

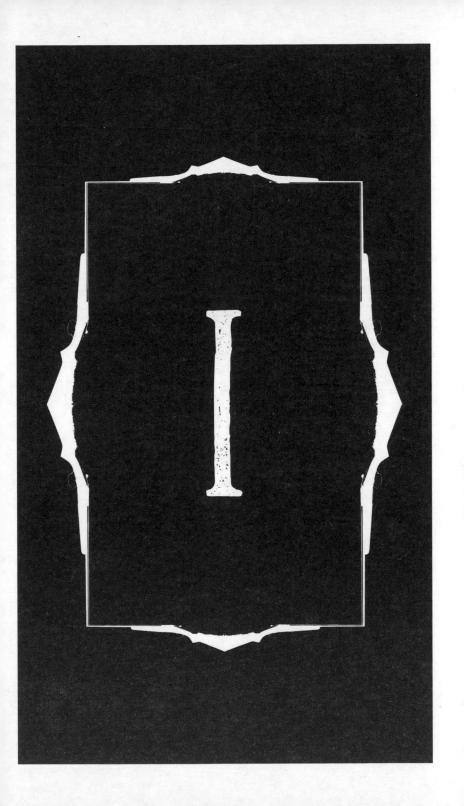

IRELAND

'The gun that I fire today will be the starting gun for civil war ...'

When Tommy Shelby breaks open a stolen crate he believes to contain cigarettes, and instead finds a consignment of British Army machine guns, he inadvertently finds himself caught up in a conflict that ultimately reshaped the United Kingdom.

On Easter Sunday in 1916, at the height of the First World War, an insurrection took place in Dublin led by Irish Republicans opposed to British rule. They took over key buildings, declaring independence for Ireland. In response, the British Army sent in over sixteen thousand troops. They faced armed rebels bedded in across the city. Just over a week of fighting took place, with the heavy artillery bombardment destroying many buildings, until the insurgents finally gave in. Over three thousand rebels were arrested, with many jailed and the leaders executed.

Though the uprising itself had not met with wide public backing in Ireland, given that many family members were serving as soldiers in the war, the hard-line British response galvanised support. In particular, it strengthened allegiance to the nationalist political party, Sinn Fein.

At the 1918 General Election, on a manifesto that promised to pull out from Westminster and set up an independent parliament in Dublin, Sinn Fein won just over half their targeted seats. This was considered to be a significant victory in the push for Ireland – a predominantly Catholic country – to break away from the United Kingdom. Even so, there remained strong support for the union in parts of the north-east (often known as Ulster), which had a significant Protestant community.

In 1919, as the Peaky Blinders began to expand their business interests in Birmingham, Sinn Fein made a significant move by declaring Ireland's independence from the United Kingdom. The party created a government and installed a new police and legal system, while a voluntary military wing formed, called the Irish Republican Army (IRA). This led to a guerrilla conflict with British forces known as the Irish War of Independence. In a period marked by great animosity and bloodshed, Irish Sinn Fein nationalists fought with British paramilitaries – known as the Black and Tans – who were drafted in to support the Royal Irish Constabulary. Finally, in 1921, a ceasefire and treaty ended British rule in all of Ireland except for the north-east of the island.

In recognition of strong support in the region from unionists, who wanted to remain in the United Kingdom, and despite deep misgivings that split the IRA, it was agreed that six counties in Ulster should be partitioned. The newly created country or province was called Northern Ireland, and remained part of the United Kingdom. It wasn't until 1948, however, that the British government formally recognised the Republic of Ireland.

In *Peaky Blinders*, the consignment of machine-guns that falls into Tommy Shelby's hands coincides with the early phase of the Irish War of Independence. The IRA approach Shelby about acquiring the weapons for use in their campaign against the British in Ireland as they seek what was often called Home Rule.

In the later phase of the war, splits appeared within the IRA between those in favour of the treaty and those opposed to it. Tommy is dragged into the growing divide when pro-treaty IRA representative, Irene O'Donnell, blackmails him into killing a blacksmith and Irish dissident to advance her aims.

Tommy carries out the assassination, aware that the might of the IRA could otherwise crush his family business. He then discovers that Major Campbell is in cahoots with O'Donnell. The sole interest of Campbell – an Ulsterman who outwardly shows a degree of contempt for pro-independence Catholic Irish, often referring to them as Fenians – is to use his knowledge of the killing as leverage against Tommy. This forces the Peaky Blinder to undertake what is basically a deep-state mission to frame the IRA in a bid to further manipulate public opinion in favour of the treaty.

Working as an agent of the British Military Service, effectively doing Sir Winston Churchill's dirty work, Tommy sets out to assassinate a high-ranking officer from the Black and Tans at the Epsom Races. As he writes in a letter to the *New York Times*, to be sent in the event of his death, the killing is intended to further fracture support for independence in Ireland and bring the country back into line with the Union.

At the same time, Campbell secretly musters men from the Ulster Volunteers to kill Tommy once he's carried out the hit. This pro-union paramilitary organisation from Campbell's native homeland was fiercely opposed to the IRA and the prospect of Home Rule. Known as the Red Hand – or Red Right Hand – for their ruthless and bloody killings, members of the Ulster Volunteers seize Tommy at a race meeting and prepare to execute him for his crimes against the state.

His life is saved, however, when one of his assailants turns his gun on the other two and reveals himself to be an undercover agent working for Churchill. Tommy's life has been spared, he learns, because Churchill has plans for him that go way beyond the future of Ireland.

JAZZ

'It's what they call music these days, brother.'

The Eden Club isn't the only place where the sound of jazz reaches Arthur's ears. When he walks through the doors of the Garrison with Finn, renovated after the IRA bombing and with the opening night in full swing, he finds himself in a new age. The sawdust and spittoons have gone, and instead high stools line the bar and velvet drapes frame the window. As for the partygoers, dressed up to celebrate, there's a mood of high spirits and sophistication in the air, and this is reflected in the new genre of music blaring from the gramophone.

Jazz was considered unsuitable listening in establishment circles when it first reached the United Kingdom from America. It had emerged in the States from a melting pot of musical styles and ethnic and cultural influences, coinciding with 1920s Prohibition. As the music of choice in underground drinking dens, the distinctive sound was often associated with illicit and hedonistic behaviour, which makes it the ideal soundtrack for a Peaky Blinders-run pub hell-bent on coming back stronger.

As Tommy Shelby surveys the scene, a ragtime tune epitomises the high spirits of the evening. Later, when the Peaky Blinders claim a table at Charles 'Darby' Sabini's Eden Club, a live jazz trio play at full tilt to a packed dance floor. This is music as an energy that's primed to incite the high life.

By the mid-1920s, jazz had taken Britain by storm. It made household names of musicians such as Duke

Ellington and Louis Armstrong, introduced a largely African-American heritage to a white European audience, and served as the soundtrack for a post-war society.

JEWELLERY

'May I just say that I might just stay here and starve to death, and choke on sapphires ...'

When Alfie Solomons sets eyes on the treasures in the Romanovs' strongroom, the gemstones, silver and gold on display illuminate his face. At a moment in history when the world was emerging from the darkness and privation of a world war, a sparkle of diamonds could only dazzle and draw all kinds of attention. At the same time, the rise of the Peaky Blinders coincided with a trend for colour in necklaces, bracelets, rings and brooches, along with a design era that transformed the face of modern life.

Emerging just before the First World War, and then dominating the 1920s and into the 30s, Art Deco celebrated modernity and sleek craftsmanship over the historical trend for flaunting wealth. Its influence can be seen in architecture of the time, from New York skyscrapers such as the Chrysler Building to decorative arts like furniture, interior design, fashion and jewellery.

The flapper movement of the decade embraced Art Deco in terms of styling, and this is evident in the long strings of continuous beads or pearls, lariat necklaces with tassels or drops, and glittering brooches and bracelets. Jewellery featuring more affordable materials such as sequins, rhinestones and polished glass was also popular, which opened up the market from what had been an elite preserve. The bib necklace, worn close against the throat, became a feature, from which hung precious or semi-precious stones such as jade or coral, while the fashion for short hair and cloche hats proved the perfect complement to dangling drop earrings.

In keeping with the trend away from visible opulence towards modernity, diamonds and other precious stones tended to be cut in new, sleek ways. A typical Art Deco ring might feature a square or oval stone, for example, as opposed to the traditional rose style with its domed, peaked top. With the emphasis on contrasting colours and clean, geometric lines, 1920s jewellery proved to be a fundamental shift from the more curved, feminine, exotic and ostentatious style of the Edwardian era that preceded it.

In *Peaky Blinders*, jewellery isn't just worn as a mark of contemporary sophistication. In 1919 and the early 1920s, Polly Gray's antique rings and necklaces might well have been passed down through generations. They represent her Gypsy heritage.

For Grace Shelby the emerald necklace she wears on her final birthday carries a darker, seemingly inescapable significance. With great glee, the exiled Russian princess, Tatiana Petrovna, tells Tommy that the glittering blue jewel he presented his wife with as a gift has in fact been cursed, and with this being a common Gypsy practice, Tommy has no reason to dismiss the claim. Moments later, an assassin's bullet meant for him strikes Grace instead. Grief-stricken, he takes the emerald to Gypsy seer Bethany Boswell, he leaves the stone with her. A token of love has for him become a symbol of heartbreak. For a jewel worth a fortune, he has paid the highest price.

BILLY KIMBER AND THE BIRMINGHAM GANG

'Nobody works with me. People work for me.'

The real Billy Kimber outlived his fictional character, shot dead by Tommy Shelby during a gang face-off in front of the Garrison, but his on-screen reputation as a feared gangster is very much based on fact.

Born in Birmingham in 1882, William 'Billy' Kimber made his mark using both brains and brawn. An accomplished street fighter and quick thinker with ambition, he rose to become head of a gang with race-course racketeering interests that reached beyond the Midlands.

The Birmingham Gang's success in this field was largely down to the Betting Act of 1853, which restricted licensed gambling to racetracks. The rising popularity of daytime excursion tickets by train also contributed, for huge numbers of people consequently flocked to the races to place bets with the bookmakers, who were quickly targeted by Kimber and his men for 'protection'. The gang stopped at nothing to ensure compliance, with disputes often settled using knuckle-dusters and razors.

A calculating and strategic thinker, Billy Kimber expanded his underworld empire by forming allegiances with some rival gangs. In building his interests, he came to arrangements with London underworld players such as Charles 'Wag' McDonald, head of the Elephant and Castle Mob. This effectively strengthened Kimber's hand in the struggle with two other gangland kingpins portrayed in the Peaky Blinders underworld – Alf Solomon and Charles 'Darby' Sabini

– for control of the major racecourses in the south of England, as well as of the burgeoning nightclub scene.

While Kimber had aligned himself with the Elephant and Castle Mob in a bid to win the Racecourse War, Sabini recruited Solomon and his Jewish gang to back him. The dispute escalated dramatically in 1921 when Kimber was shot and injured outside Sabini's London flat, where he had gone to negotiate with his rival. Solomon was arrested and charged with the shooting, but found not guilty when Kimber and his associates played by the criminals' code and refused to testify.

In 1927, after years of conflict and short-lived truces with Charles 'Darby' Sabini's gang in the fight for control of the racecourses, Billy Kimber took flight from the UK for America following a shooting incident at a London pub favoured by his rival. On his return to England in 1929, Kimber found that opportunities at the premier racecourses had diminished. Efforts by the police and the Jockey Club of Britain to clean up betting practices persuaded the veteran racketeer to make his money from less regulated and more informal horse racing. Little is known of his later years until 1945, when he died in a Torquay nursing home at the age of sixty-three. In his will, Billy Kimber left his widow more than three and a half thousand pounds, which was a considerable sum of money at the time.

KING GEORGE V

'We went through hell for our king. Walked through the flames of war ...'

Though heads of state are sometimes portrayed as presiding over their subjects with lofty detachment, it could be said that the character of King George V in *Peaky Blinders* considers some to serve a useful purpose. Right from the beginning, he has a connection with a Birmingham street gang leader that becomes increasingly entangled as the story unfolds.

Tommy Shelby and the reigning monarch of the era might not meet in person, and yet they come to depend on each other for matters of the utmost importance. Tommy's covert missions serve the interests of the establishment, from hastening the Irish treaty to enabling Britain's intervention in Russian politics, and ultimately he has to rely on royal intervention to save his family from the noose.

The grandson of Queen Victoria, King George V, took the throne of the United Kingdom from 1910 until his death in 1936. His reign saw major events take place, such as Ireland's bid for independence, the First World War and the Suffragette Movement that gave women the right to vote.

Throughout this tumultuous period in Britain's history, the king was regarded in high esteem by the people. A man with a strong sense of duty, he served as a unifying force, engendering a strong sense of patriotism. With this national mood in mind, just a year after the end of the war, Tommy organises a public burning of pictures of George V, which were commonly found hung in homes, pubs and civic buildings at the time. He invites the press to cover this wilfully provocative protest, which is in response to the arrival in the city of Chief Inspector Campbell and his men. Campbell has been tasked with tracking down stolen machine-guns, acquired inadvertently by the Peaky Blinders and which Tommy intends to use to his advantage. As a war veteran, Tommy tells the attending journalist that it's a symbolic action intended to spare the king from witnessing the harassment endured by his countrymen in Small Heath at the hands of 'these new coppers over from Belfast'.

Aware of the respect afforded to the crown at the time, Tommy knows the story will be spiked by the Secretary of State, Sir Winston Churchill. As Churchill is also responsible for ordering Chief Inspector Campbell and his men to Birmingham, Tommy's signal to Whitehall is intended to protect his own interests. It's a bold, strategic move that quietly brings the king into the frame, where he remains throughout the story of the Peaky Blinders' ascendency to a very different throne.

LANCHESTER MOTOR COMPANY

'This is business . . .'

When Tommy Shelby first strides across the factory floor at this Sparkbrook vehicle plant, the smoke, sparks and plumes of flames look more like a scene from hell than a production line. In the 1920s, an age before automation, car manufacturing was physical and labour-intensive work. For marques such as Lanchester, it helped to earn a reputation for prestige and innovation in the fledgling automobile market – with a sideline in providing the military with armoured vehicles.

An early incarnation of what would become the Lanchester Motor Company was founded in 1899 by three brothers, George, Frank and Frederick – the latter being an innovative engineer of his time. In 1895, just ten years after Karl Benz famously patented the world's first wheeled motor vehicle, Frederick built a one-cylinder, five-horsepower model that, for the brothers, served as a vision of the future. Several further prototypes followed before the company established a factory in Birmingham and went into full-time production.

Frederick Lanchester's next significant achievement was to produce the first mass-market disc brake. This helped to grow the company's reputation as a manufacturer of well-designed cars that delivered a smooth ride.

Like many British factories during the First World War, Lanchester repurposed its production line to support the military effort. The company switched

135

from manufacturing cars to making munitions and aeroplane engines, but perhaps most notably produced the Lanchester Armoured Car. This turreted vehicle, built on the chassis of Lanchester's popular Sporting Fury Luxury Tourer, proved to be popular with the army. It was relatively fast and handled well across a variety of terrains, from the arctic to the desert.

In his covert work for the British establishment, which told him they were quietly assisting resistance against the new Soviet regime in Russia, Tommy agrees to steal a number of armoured cars from the Lanchester Motor Factory. On his first visit he finds them stored under tarpaulin, mothballed after the war, and he subsequently devises a plan to smuggle them by train to the port.

Despite several twists and turns in the mission, which result in the armoured cars being spread across the tracks in a tangled heap of metal, Tommy's involvement with Lanchester continues. Later, as a factory owner himself, he listens to union activist Jessie Eden recite a list of holdings owned by Shelby Company Limited that includes the Birmingham car manufacturer. While Tommy Shelby's name never appeared on the list of directors in real life, the Lanchester Motor Company thrived during the 1920s, producing luxury cars, only to fall victim to the down-turn in the economy following the 1929 Wall Street Crash.

Forced into liquidation, the company was purchased at a rock-bottom price by BSA (the Birmingham Small Arms Company), which owned the next-door factory and needed to expand. As a result, the Lanchester marque was absorbed into its sister subsidiary, Daimler, and production moved to Coventry. Its focus on high-end, luxury vehicles appealed to owners such as King George VI, who was said to favour his car over comparative models by Rolls-Royce. The final Lanchester model left the production line in the mid-1950s before Daimler, and the marque that was once the pride of Birmingham's automotive industry, was purchased from BSA by the British car giant of the time, Jaguar.

LAYERING

'Tommy, I'm fucking freezing here.'

In a decade known for its move towards simplicity in fashion – particularly in womenswear as celebrated by the shapeless drop-waist dress of the flapper – the Peaky Blinders made a virtue of dressing in layers.

For Tommy Shelby and his associates, living in Small Heath just before central heating became a feature of domestic homes, clothing wasn't just about style. As Lizzie discovers to her cost during a canal-side tryst with Tommy, it's also about insulating against the cold. In order to tick both boxes, people opted for layers of thin clothing that would keep them snug out on the cobbled streets, and that could be easily removed in front of a crackling fire.

A penny collar shirt and woollen or tweed waistcoat is central to the Peaky Blinders layered approach. It looks both traditional and smart, with or without a jacket, and also works with the addition of a heavy overcoat should conditions outside prove hostile.

LIMEHOUSE

'I told Finn to stay out of it. He obviously didn't listen ...'

The scattering of narrow passages that forms the oriental quarter of 1919 Birmingham in *Peaky Blinders* is nothing compared to London's sprawling Chinatown in Limehouse a decade later. Here, Aberama Gold, Isaiah and Finn comb through a warren of narrow alleys, bustling markets strung with lanterns, basements, back rooms and cramped boarding houses in order to carry out a hit for Tommy Shelby.

A district in the east end of the capital, on the north bank of the River Thames, Limehouse grew from its relationship with the waterway. Sailors disembarked here through the centuries, patronising drinking establishments, while trades popped up to service the maritime industry. In the late 1800s, the area became home to a small but steadily growing Chinese community. These were traders who had made the journey by sea and then settled, bringing with them a strong sense of identity and culture.

During the early years of the twentieth century, the Chinese presence in Limehouse was often met with distrust, ignorance and prejudice. An air of caution and mystery surrounded the existence of a Confucian temple, while exaggerated and unverified tales of crime rings and opium dens earned the district a reputation as a dangerous quarter. It's here that the infamous drug dealer of the age, and *Peaky Blinders* character, Brilliant Chang, gave louche drug parties before his arrest, imprisonment and subsequent disappearance into underworld folklore. His story – and the area – is said to have inspired Sax Rohmer's *The Adventures of Dr Fu Manchu* series, further casting Limehouse as an alien enclave within a familiar world. Following the Second World War, in which the district suffered heavy bombing, the community relocated to Soho. Responding to the growing taste for Far East cuisine, many opened restaurants, bakeries and grocery stores, which steadily grew in number to become the Chinatown that exists today.

LINERS

'I have contacts. People in Cunard and Liverpool.'

Throughout the story of the Peaky Blinders, the docks at Liverpool serve as a gateway to opportunity as much as an escape to a new life in the United States of America.

For Vicente Changretta and his wife, standing nervously in the queue for embarkation before Tommy's men catch them, making it to the ship's ramp is literally a matter of life and death. Freddie Thorne rejects Polly's invitation to make the crossing with his new bride, Ada, Tommy's father takes off for Boston having made a fleeting visit to fleece the family of funds, while Arthur and Linda quite literally miss the boat on account of being arrested for sedition and murder. Grace Burgess sails to America successfully, only to return in the wake of a doomed first marriage, and Michael Gray does likewise having scuppered the Shelby Company fortunes in the Wall Street Crash. Liverpool is also the point of arrival for New York mobster Luca Changretta, who has come to avenge the death of his father at the hands of Tommy Shelby before he could present his boarding pass.

In the wake of the First World War, the ocean liner enjoyed a golden age. As the economy recovered – along with a sense of optimism – people were keen to expand their horizons. Undeterred by the sinking of the *Titanic* in 1912, the transatlantic passage from the UK to America embodied such hopes and dreams.

In the 1920s, almost one hundred years since the first steamship had successfully completed the journey, the great liners that sailed back and forth were feats of engineering as much as design, style and glamour. The ships provided opulent first-class luxury and also cheaper steerage class for the huge number of people emigrating to America in search of fortune. Docks such as Liverpool and Southampton were regularly crowded with passengers, well-wishers and people who simply wished to witness these elegant giants of the ocean set sail – not just for America but for ports around the world, for example in South Africa, Australia, India and the Far East.

As Tommy Shelby expanded his business empire from the UK to America, the Atlantic Ocean was dominated by two passenger lines, White Star and Cunard, as well as growing competition from French- and German-owned ships. In this highly commercial world, competitors chased the prestigious Blue Riband; an unofficial annual award for the fastest crossing. Passengers could choose from different classes of travel, and expect to be at sea for between just four to five days.

By the 1930s, the duration for making the crossing had come down to a little over three days, and yet the sun was about to set on the popularity of the transatlantic liner. The Great Depression vastly cut down the number of travellers to America, causing financial problems for the industry and leading to the merger of Cunard and White Star. Then, during the Second World War, ships were requisitioned and many sunk in enemy attacks, with great loss of life. Post-war, the ocean liners found themselves competing with a new form of travel. The commercial aviation industry took off in the 1950s and its popularity continued to climb. A decade later, with passenger demand all but gone and ocean-going interest turning to the cruise ship, the remaining liners of the golden age made their last commercial voyages.

LITTLE ITALY

'He's going around Nechells saying he's going to kill you.'

When Polly warns John that Luca Changretta's son, Angel, is unhappy about being told to stay away from Lizzie Stark by order of the Peaky Blinders, he doesn't take the threat seriously. Not only does John consider him to be a hothead he can easily handle, but he also knows Angel is sounding off to people close to his home turf.

Little Italy is located just a few miles south, in Digbeth, close to the railways that have always brought immigrants to cities in search of a new life. The relationship between Italians and Birmingham dates back to the nineteenth century, when traders who had ventured all the way from cities such as Rome and

Naples opted to settle down in the Midlands instead of making the arduous return journey. Many followed for economic reasons, following famine and rising prices back home.

Over time, the growing community introduced a taste of the old country to the city by opening small businesses and notably earning a reputation as a place to buy ice cream. It's into this enclave that Danny Whizz-Bang blunders on the cusp of a psychotic episode from the war. He trips over chairs outside the Travelli Café beside Giovanni's bicycle shop, and then reacts with tragic consequences when the Italian owner steps out with a knife in hand. The stabbing to death of the man at Danny's hands leads his family to approach Tommy seeking retribution, which he stages in a way that spares the life of his old comrade. He may have saved Danny from a bullet to the back of the head, but this incident is just a taste of the often-volatile relationship to come between the Peaky Blinders and the Italians as the story deepens.

 ## LONDON

'Just smoke and trouble.'

As Tommy Shelby's business ambitions grow beyond Birmingham, the capital becomes the next significant step on the ladder to his empire. London is no place for a Gypsy according to Esme, but nothing can deter Tommy from his grand design.

In *Peaky Blinders*, London is the home of Alfie Solomons and his bootlegging operation, as well as Charles 'Darby' Sabini's Eden Club, where Tommy, his brother and their foot-soldiers raise hell to stamp their authority and claim the place as their own. Ada moves here on her return from Shelby Company business in America, and as Tommy enters politics so the capital becomes a second home for him.

London is a well-known city, familiar to many, but what was it really like there at a time of rum-smuggling and protection rackets, high society and slums? In 1919, the country was still reeling from being on a war footing for four years. Unemployment was high, while industry that had run at full tilt during the First World War, such as coal mining and steel-making, went into decline. In a city that relied on service industries rather than heavy manufacturing, however, and that had excellent transport links via rail and sea, London escaped the full impact of this downturn.

Despite the economic challenges across the country, Londoners set out to make the most of life in post-war society. Demobilisation had seen men return from the frontline to their former lives, and while some struggled to adapt after their wartime experiences, others were keen to seize the opportunities that peacetime afforded.

When Tommy and his brothers enter the Eden Club for the very first time, the hedonistic scenes of sex, drugs, drinking and dancing capture something of the mood among the capital's young and liberal, aristocratic and wealthy classes at the time. Women had just received the right to vote, and as the Roaring Twenties took off, many were determined to celebrate a growing sense of independence in the jazz clubs and cocktail bars that began to open. The mood certainly turns Arthur's head as he takes over the running of the Eden Club, which earns him a warning from Tommy about the dangers of excess living when business is the priority.

The 1920s was the decade in which traffic in London began to rise. Use of horse-drawn carts and carriages dwindled as cars became commercially affordable to a mass market. And with a strong public transport network in the form of buses, trams, major railway terminals and the burgeoning underground system, the capital increasingly became a hive of activity. For many, such as Esme Shelby or a narrowboat man like Charlie Strong, who delivers his goods by the old waterway from Birmingham and then makes the slow return via the same means, the pace of life there is all too much. For others, like Tommy Shelby, London stands at the frontier of possibilities. The capital is a place of hopes and dreams as much as pitfalls and danger, and for a Peaky Blinder going places, it's all there for the taking.

THE LUCAS FACTORY

'*Apparently, all the female factory workers in the city are joining the protest in sympathy.*'

In the Peaky Blinders story, the workforce at this Birmingham car parts factory in Sparkhill, a neighbouring area to Small Heath, counts on union activist Jessie Eden to represent their interests. She's effective in her role, campaigning for much better working conditions and equal pay for women. In 1924, Eden first comes to Tommy Shelby's attention by calling out the female workers from several sections and encouraging other women to strike in solidarity – including those from the Shelby Company Limited.

Much of the background storyline for the character of Jessie Eden mirrors the life of the woman she's based upon. Serving as a shop steward, Eden really did work at the Lucas Car Factory in Sparkhill, and mobilised the workforce on several significant occasions to take strike action.

Founded in the 1850s by Joseph Lucas, the company expanded over the decades from making pressed metal products such as buckets and plant-pot holders to automotive electrical components. By the 1920s, the Joseph Lucas Motor Components Factory had become a major employer in the area, and a focal point in Birmingham for equal pay. As a representative for the Transport and General Workers Union, Jessie Eden was instrumental in leading not just the small but significant walk-out by women from two sections of the factory over equal pay, but also in rallying workers during the 1926 General Strike. Most notably, Eden was responsible for industrial action by ten thousand women at the plant in 1931 over what were regarded as unreasonable productivity measures. The actions of Jessie Eden and the women from the Lucas factory are said to have significantly contributed to the mass unionisation of female workers across the UK.

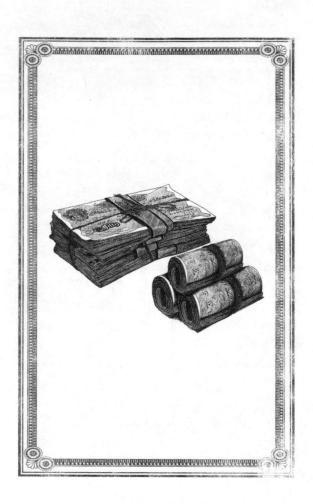

MAFIA

'Arthur, have you looked at your post?'

When every member of the Shelby family receives a letter from New York City bearing the imprint of a hand in black ink, they know enough about Mafia custom to recognise they've effectively received a death sentence.

The black hand, sent by the mobster Luca Changretta, is intended as notice that he is set to avenge the death of his father, Vicente, by the Peaky Blinders. The vendetta is enough to rattle John, Arthur and Polly, and prompts Tommy to put a plan together in the hope that it will save their lives.

During the 1920s and 30s, the America Mafia – or 'The Mob' – were both feared and revered on both sides of the Atlantic. The organisation evolved in the late 1800s from a loose collective of street gangs made up of Italian immigrants. Many had former lives or links with the Sicilian Mafia in Italy, or 'the old country', though as time passed the American outfit would come to control its own activities.

The American Mafia emerged principally from New York ghettos like Harlem – which was also known as Italian Harlem – and an enclave called Little Italy in Manhattan. At the turn of the century, it was estimated that upwards of half a million Italians had arrived in New York in search of a better life. While the vast majority were law abiding, a minority formed territorial gangs that turned to low-level criminal activities to make money. As well as indulging in petty crimes, some turned to extortion by sending letters to their victims demanding money to spare them from kidnap or physical harm. To identify themselves, they adorned the letters with the drawing of a hand print in thick black ink. These were sometimes decorated with symbols such as a knife or hangman's noose, and became known as '*La Mano Nera*', or 'Black Hand Letter'. Such was the fear they aroused that some saw them as a curse that could only be lifted by complying with the demands made in them. On occasions, the motive for serving a Black Hand went beyond extortion threats, as the Peaky Blinders would discover for themselves.

In the early years of the twentieth century, as power struggles took place, many local gangs that practised the Black Hand started to join together and strengthen in number. The Five Points Gang was one of the most prominent of the times. It emerged in New York with some sense of hierarchy, and included young street hoodlums who would go on to become powerful crime bosses, such as Lucky Luciano, Johnny Torrio and Al Capone.

As the Big Apple gangs began to merge, their criminal activities continued to revolve around Black Hand Letters and protection rackets, while also expanding to take in gambling, control of prostitution rings and money laundering. Just as the Five Points Gang began to control Italian criminal enterprises in New York, other gangs stamped their authority on major American cities such as New Orleans and Chicago. Regional and national fights for dominance continued into the 1910s, until slowly a country-wide organisation took shape.

Collectively, the American Mafia (also known as Cosa Nostra, like the Italian organisation) operated under strict codes. Each 'family' within it came under the rule of a mob boss and had a descending system of rank. Joining the Mafia was heavily ritualised. Men of Italian heritage deemed suitable were 'made', and swore a lifelong oath of loyalty and silence about their activities. A made man, fully initiated into the American Mafia, started out as a foot-soldier. With time, he could earn promotion by showing commitment, a fierce sense of respect and willingness to follow any instruction from on high that served the interests of the organisation. By the time Luca Changretta makes the crossing from New York to Liverpool, having pledged to kill the Shelby family for taking his father's life, he brings Mafia soldiers under his command.

It was the advent of Prohibition in the 1920s, and the opportunities this presented for supplying the country's underground demand for alcohol, that saw the American Mafia's business enterprises expand massively. This was accompanied by a growing reputation for brutality, violence and an unflinching commitment to settling scores. Wise to the potential consequences of crossing The Mob, it's no surprise that Tommy makes urgent preparations to protect his family ahead of Changretta's arrival in Birmingham.

After the end of Prohibition in 1933, the American Mafia refocused their efforts on running protection rackets and money laundering, with drug-trafficking, loan sharking and infiltrating labour unions to exploit both the workforce and employers. Mob bosses even established a central governing body called The Commission to maintain order in what had become an organisation comprising more than twenty crime families – with five in New York alone. From the 1930s to the 1960s, efforts to curb The Mob's activities were regularly foiled by the organisation through bribery, intimidation and murder.

The fightback again Mafia activities began in the 1960s, notably led by the US Attorney General Robert Kennedy, the younger brother of President John F. Kennedy. It wasn't, though, until the 1970s that the government began to seriously curb the might of the American Mafia. Recruiting spies and informers allowed law enforcement agencies to gain critical intelligence, but true legal empowerment came with the introduction of the Racketeer Influenced and Corrupt Organisation Act (RICO). The main purpose of this law was to allow the government to go after not just Mafia foot-soldiers who undertook illegal activities, but The Mob bosses who issued the orders and profited from any proceeds. Over the decades that followed, with the additional ability to seize assets, prosecutors succeeded in taking down several prominent crime families.

By the turn of the twenty-first century, with many prominent mob players imprisoned or in witness-protection programmes, having acted as informants, the American Mafia was unrecognisable compared to the organisation that ruled the underworld one hundred years before. Mafia families, however, are still believed to be in operation in some regions of the USA, and the image of the sharp-suited wise guy with a tommy gun in hand has become an icon of underworld history.

MARGATE

'I saw this beautiful house down in Margate . . . a piece of Heaven, actually.'

When Alfie reveals his plans to retire, facing Tommy in the dressing room at the boxing hall before the fight gets into full swing, he paints a picture of his own personal paradise. The Jewish gangster describes a white building with an impressive view of the earth's curvature and a monkey puzzle tree outside – a species that proved popular at the turn of the century after first being imported from Chile in the 1850s. It's a particular and passionate pitch, and a reflection of just how smitten Alfie Solomons has become with a historic seaside town.

Margate is situated on the Kent coast to the east of London. Overlooking the English Channel, with Dover to the south, it was one of the medieval confederation of five ports – known as Cinque Ports – that harboured the royal ships and ensured they were battle-ready. Although that role became redundant over time, Margate became one of the first coastal towns to cater for the rising popularity of saltwater bathing. With its close proximity to the capital, visitors travelled there from the late eighteenth century onwards to enjoy what was commonly believed to be the restorative effects of sun, sea and sand.

With the advent of the railways, Margate developed as a popular resort. What had been a small harbour with a cluster of houses became the site for lodgings, crescent buildings and hotels as well as seafront villas, complete with balcony, like the one that bewitches

Alfie Solomons. Bathing rooms, a theatre and library all added to the sense that Margate catered for both leisure and culture; a place for the wealthy to unwind.

Notably, Margate was home to the Royal Sea Bathing Hospital. This was one of the first specialist infirmaries dedicated to using sea bathing, sunshine and fresh air in the treatment of patients suffering from scrofula (tuberculosis of the joints, glands and bones). When Alfie Solomons claims to be dying from cancer, expressing the wish to end his days in peace at the resort, the medical expertise on hand in the town might well have strengthened his decision to move to what was a prestigious location at the time of the Peaky Blinders.

Margate continued to expand between the wars. In the 1920s, with the addition of an amusement park proving to be a major attraction, the town rivalled Brighton and Blackpool in popularity. As with so many British resorts, however, the rise of cheap flights and overseas package holidays in the 1960s and 70s saw the town's tourist industry go into decline. Following redevelopment efforts in the 1990s, which included the establishment of the Turner Contemporary art gallery, Margate has enjoyed a cultural renaissance in recent years. With his critical eye and appreciation of craftsmanship, no doubt a man like Alfie Solomons would approve.

THE MARQUIS OF LORNE

'He's Polly Shelby's son! Are you fucking suicidal?'

When Isaiah Jesus receives a racist and hostile welcome from the locals in this Birmingham pub, having walked in for a drink with Michael, the pair are drawn into a brutal fist fight. It's only when the main aggressor registers what the landlord has been trying to communicate to him that he backs off in fear. By now, however, the damage is done, or at least it will be when Arthur and John visit to torch the place in retribution.

The event may be a work of fiction, but the Marquis of Lorne pub was real, situated to the north of Small Heath. The building dates back to the late 1800s, and though the façade and interior have undergone alterations over time, it remains standing as a pub under a different name.

The Guns is another Small Heath drinking establishment that falls under the protective wing of the Peaky Blinders. Given the presence of the Birmingham Small Arms Company in Small Heath, located off Armoury Road, it's no surprise to learn that a pub called the Gunmakers Arms – also known as The Gunners of The Guns – once served a thirsty workforce nearby.

MATCHBOX

'There are cigarettes in my pocket ... and matches.'

For a man rarely seen without a cigarette, Tommy Shelby always has the means to light one to hand. Small, portable cigarette lighters came into existence at the turn of the twentieth century, but they didn't become widely available until the 1920s. It was the invention of the Zippo a decade later that saw the lighter become mainstream. Even then, smokers could always rely on the striking of the humble match to light their cigarettes and cigars, and Shelby and his family are no exception.

When Tommy pits himself against Billy Kimber and then Charles Sabini, a box of matches at the time was pretty much a compulsory item in every smoker's pocket. At the turn of the twentieth century, shortly after the development of mass production, smoking had never been more popular. With the health issues associated with tobacco not widely recognised until the second half of the century, the story of the Peaky Blinders takes place in an era when it often seemed like everyone had a cigarette within reach.

Each time Tommy strikes a match against the side of the box, he does so safe in the knowledge that it won't produce a shower of sparks or cause him toxic harm. The concept of the safety match had been in existence since the middle of the nineteenth century, but this only transformed the way it ignited. It wasn't until the late 1800s that action was taken to halt the use of a chemical substance contained in the match-head called white phosphorus. Most notably, the production process caused serious health issues among workers at the match factories in the form of necrosis of the jaw.

In 1888, the predominantly female workforce at the Bryant & May factory in Bow, East London, came out on strike. With many suffering from this disfiguring condition, which was also known as 'phossy face' or 'phossy jaw', the strikers attracted a great deal of public attention as well as outrage at their plight. The strike ended when management pledged to address their concerns about working conditions, and then sought to replace the use of white phosphorus with a more expensive but ultimately safer red variety – contained not in the match-head but in the striking surface.

In 1910, having recognised the dangers inherent in using white phosphorus in match-heads, the government banned its use in match production completely. Just under a decade later, when Tommy Shelby lights a cigarette, he does so using a safety match and box, the concept of which we still recognise today.

In a competitive market among smokers at the turn of the century, matchbox manufacturer's quickly saw the potential for their product to stand out on the shelves through attractive packaging. As a result, the matchbox sleeve became a canvas for striking designs, typography and artistry, many of which are considered collector's items today. At the time of the Peaky Blinders, Swedish manufacturers dominated the market, along with common British names such as Bryant & May, which produced the Swan Vesta brand. This familiar strike-anywhere match would go on to become a bestseller in the 1930s, and continued to compete with the emergence of the cigarette lighter.

MEDIUM

'Let's begin. Hands on the table ...'

Desperate to learn the fate of her long-lost daughter, Polly visits a woman at her terraced house after dark who claims to communicate with the spirit world. By invitation of the medium, Mrs Price, she takes her place alongside several other customers longing to speak with loved ones, and leaves elated. In the cold light of the next day, however, it's Esme who explains how the woman has tricked her, which is the last thing Polly wants to hear.

Throughout history, there have always been both individuals and cultures claiming to be able to communicate with the dead. In the early decades of the twentieth century, particularly in the UK and America, the spirit medium was a familiar figure considered to be both a source of insight and entertainment. Such was the appetite among the public that those who set up as mediums – such as 'Mrs Price from the Patch' – could earn a healthy income from their services.

The attraction of visiting a spirit medium stemmed from the rising popularity of the Ouija board in the mid- to late 1800s. This was a particular favourite among the upper classes. As well as an entertainment, it was a means of flirting with a realm considered by some to be within the bounds of science at the time. Famous names such as Sir Arthur Conan Doyle were fully invested in the concept of life after death, endorsing several self-proclaimed psychics of the day. Such figures also created an air of legitimacy that would go on to draw often vulnerable clients from across the social spectrum. By 1919, in a country wreathed in grief having lost so many young men on the battlefield, those who opened their doors as mediums could expect a steady custom. Often, the practitioner would gather a number of people in one session, known as a seance, which arguably heightened the atmosphere and willingness to believe when the medium went on to conjure messages from the dead.

Psychics through the 1920s practised a variety of methods to enable their clientele to feel they were communicating with another realm. Cold reading often occurred before the session commenced, in which the psychic assessed their client's hopes and expectations from the session simply by observing everything from their manner to their clothing, and response to seemingly innocent questions. A deft practitioner could uncover all the information they needed to deliver a satisfying outcome.

In *Peaky Blinders*, Mrs Price employs a common practice among mediums of inviting everyone around the table to place their hands upon a glass, which appears to move in response to her questions. Through history, others seemingly summon lost loved ones by speaking in tongues or voices, or peer into a crystal ball to divine messages from the afterlife.

With their long-held and strong beliefs in the spirit world, and perceived air of mystique, mediums from the Gypsy community found their services in demand from outsiders. For some Travellers, this could prove a fruitful source of income as they moved through the countryside. The image of the Gypsy seer peering into her crystal ball in her caravan – while a client looked on spellbound – has long been a common and alluring stereotype.

Towards the end of the 1920s, it's believed that almost a quarter of a million individuals in the UK claimed to have the gift of communicating with the spirit world. Mediums were regularly invited to perform at spiritualist meetings, much to the dismay of the Church, perpetuating the idea that the realm of the dead was somehow close at hand.

As more earthly communications improved through the 1930s, particularly between America and Britain, so infamous stories began to circulate of fraud and deceptive practices perpetrated by mediums, along with supporting evidence that could not be disproved. In *Peaky Blinders*, Esme reveals to Polly that one of Mrs Price's customers around the table was in fact her cousin, tasked with moving the glass. Polly reacts badly, of course, and indeed many believers when confronted with the facts still find it hard to accept the reality. Traumatised by her reprieve from a public execution, Polly becomes convinced that she herself has the gift and spends a year lost to her family while communing with her late daughter and hosting seances.

Despite those who placed great faith in the practice, the popularity for the spirit medium began to wane, though, ironically perhaps, none of them foresaw it, but it didn't evaporate completely. Demand still exists to this day for individuals who claim to act as a conduit between the living and the dead. Nevertheless, there's no doubt that the era of the Peaky Blinders marked a magical high point for the psychic industry.

MILD

'He's got work tomorrow. Give him only dark mild.'

In the world of *Peaky Blinders*, a pint of this often dark-coloured malty beverage stands at the opposite end of the alcohol spectrum from the Shelbys' favoured Irish whiskey. It's the drink Tommy allows young Finn at the reopening of the Garrison, having confiscated his shot glass. He also limits Michael to the very same beverage when he joins the family fold 'as he has work tomorrow'.

Mild might not be the first choice among pub regulars today, but in the early twentieth century it was a popular drink. Cheap, tasty and often not too strong – and generally served as a pint – it was enjoyed by both men and women and sometimes ordered as a chaser. While it's still available today, the popularity of mild doesn't compare to its heyday in the Peaky Blinders era.

Beer and ale are distinguished by the fermentation process and the time required to produce it. Mild is often described as a young beer with a low hop content and relatively quick ageing process. Alcohol strength varies but it tends to have a predominantly sweet, fruity or malty taste. While both beer and ale have been brewed for centuries, mild rose in popularity in the early nineteenth century and took over from a traditional dark beer called porter. Different brews of mild produced a range of colours, strengths and flavours, but the short brewing time and low production cost meant all varieties quickly became an established feature behind the bar.

Strict controls on brewing during the First World War had a severe impact on the original gravity, taste, price and subsequent popularity of mild. Following the end of the conflict in 1918, however, the drink made a comeback across the country, with a particular demand in the Midlands. There, a mix of mild and brown ale became popular, known as a 'brown and mild' or a 'boilermaker'.

Mild isn't just a drink for young Peaky Blinders, of course. Freddie Thorne breaks the Ada-related tension with Tommy by joining him at the bar and ordering a pint of the original dark stuff, just like most Garrison regulars. The taste for mild among Britain's drinkers would last until the 1960s. Then, trends moved towards bitter and lighter ales. Mild is still available behind most bars, and a discerning choice for those seeking a flavour of vintage life.

SIR OSWALD MOSLEY

'You have come to my attention . . .'

Addressing the House of Commons in his first term as MP, Tommy Shelby calls upon his experience as a man who makes things happen by speaking with great eloquence and conviction. His ability to articulate the concerns of the common worker doesn't go unnoticed by a fellow MP – a character in *Peaky Blinders* based on a real-life figure of the time who had grand designs for the future of the nation. Not only does Sir Oswald Mosley shape up to be someone who matches Tommy in strategic thinking to suit his own ends, but this architect of the British Union of Fascists even threatens to outplay him completely.

Born to an aristocratic family in 1896, Sir Oswald Ernald Mosley of Ancoats, 6th Baronet, first made his mark as a notable boxer and fencing champion at school. He attended Sandhurst Royal Military College, from which he was expelled for 'a riotous act of retaliation against a fellow cadet'. During the First World War, Mosley served for a time with the cavalry. Although he didn't represent the regiment that arrived late to rescue Tommy's besieged infantry division in the story of the Peaky Blinders, Mosley's elite military background would have been met with little respect by the Shelby brothers. Following a transfer to the Royal Flying Corps, and an accident that left him with a permanent limp, Mosley was declared unfit to fight at the front line and carried out desk work until the end of the war.

After the conflict ended in 1918, Sir Oswald Mosley turned his attention to politics. A strikingly confident young man with strong convictions, at twenty-one years of age he became the youngest person at the time to sit as an MP. Mosley represented the Conservatives, but his impatient nature and pursuit of power would lead him to undertake a journey across the political spectrum in the years that followed until the outbreak of the Second World War. This began when Mosley clashed with his own government over its handling of the Irish question. A fierce critic of the Black and Tans' conduct in fighting the IRA, the MP for Harrow ultimately left the Conservative Party to stand as an independent candidate at the 1922 General Election and win the seat.

In his private life, Sir Oswald was a confident and charismatic man with a reputation as a womaniser. In 1920 he married Lady Cynthia Curzon. The couple became a feature on the high-society calendar, while behind closed doors he allegedly conducted relationships with both his wife's younger sister and their stepmother.

Having retained his seat at the 1923 General Election, and earned a reputation as a strong, impassioned speaker, Mosley began to lean towards the left politically. This culminated in a move to Labour in 1924, who were in power at the time, but he went on to lose as a prospective MP for the party at the General Election that October.

Following a year outside politics, Mosley fought and won a by-election in Birmingham, which is where his ties to the city begin. With the Conservatives in government, he set about establishing himself as a prominent Labour parliamentarian. When the party won the General Election in 1929, however, leader Ramsay MacDonald chose not to select him for cabinet. Instead, Mosley served as the Duchy of Lancaster, which was not considered a central role and left him feeling overlooked.

For Mosley, the final straw came when his economic recovery proposals were rejected by Ramsay. Believing he was wasting his time in the government, and increasingly convinced that the country required stronger leadership, Mosley resigned in 1930 to establish The New Party. In *Peaky Blinders*, Tommy Shelby comes into his orbit around this time. Mosley sees a use for him in gathering support for his plans and Tommy seemingly complies. Secretly, he's undertaking intelligence for Sir Winston Churchill, who regards Mosley as a potential danger to the state.

A political force that revolved around its figurehead, whose confidence increased with every grassroots rally he held, Sir Oswald quickly moved his New Party towards a fascist outlook. An admirer of Mussolini's rise to power in Italy, Mosley crystallised his views in 1932 by dissolving the party and establishing the British Union of Fascists. He stoked a sense of dissatisfaction among his followers by blaming outside forces for the country's economic problems and lack of strong leadership in the government of the day. It was a deeply divisive standpoint, and Mosley's move towards extreme nationalism, coupled with the fervent support it gained in certain quarters, disgusted and alarmed many people in equal measure.

In 1933, Mosley's wife, Cynthia, died from peritonitis, after which, in 1936, Mosley married Diana Mitford, a high-society divorcee with strong social links to members of the German Nazi Party. The couple were married in secret at the house of propaganda chief Joseph Goebbels, with Adolf Hitler in attendance as a guest. By now, Mosley's admiration of the Nazi leader was evident, feeding into his development of the British Union of Fascists (BUF).

In a bid to combat protests at what were increasingly controversial rallies, Sir Oswald Mosley enrolled uniformed security known as 'blackshirts' – a nod to Hitler's notorious brownshirts as the Nazi Party strengthened in Germany. Billy Boys leader, Billy Fullerton – Jimmy McCavern in *Peaky Blinders* – provided men to marshal rallies in the north of the country. Increasingly nationalistic, anti-communist and anti-Semitic in tone, many activities involving the British Union of Fascists ended in outbreaks of violence.

Fired up by the sense of power at hand, in 1936 Mosley organised a provocative BUF march through a predominately Jewish quarter of the East End. As a measure of the political mood in the country, and despite heavy policing, the march was met by fierce resistance from member of the Jewish community (allegedly including Alf Solomon and his gang), socialists, communists, anarchists as well as anyone opposed to a troubling ideology that had taken root in countries across Europe. The Battle of Cable Street, as it famously came to be known, led to Mosley abandoning the march. Today, with the resistance commemorated by a blue plaque, it's considered to be one of the defining moments in Britain's history of anti-fascism.

It was the outbreak of the Second World War that saw Sir Oswald Mosley's vision of a fascist regime come to an end. A real-life intelligence operation, run over several years by the establishment, considered Mosley to be a credible threat to the national interest. It was widely believed that should Germany successfully invade Britain, Sir Oswald would be installed by the Nazis as leader. Interred for his political beliefs, having openly courted Hitler in the years leading up to the outbreak of the conflict, Mosley and his wife, Diana, were imprisoned from 1940 to 1943, after which he spent the rest of the war under house arrest.

In 1945, with Germany defeated, Mosley's attempts to return to the political frontline were unsuccessful. With no appetite for fascism in the UK, he found his support had withered and, in 1951, he and Diana went into self-exile in Ireland and then Paris. Retired from political life, but without remorse for his convictions, Sir Oswald Mosley died in 1980.

MOUSTACHE

'I'm Arthur fucking Shelby!'

When it comes to wearing a moustache with style, and with not a supporting beard whisker in sight, Arthur Shelby has got it covered. Right from the moment he makes his presence known, running the betting shop in Watery Lane, this is a man who is unafraid to express his character through the facial hair above his upper lip.

Arthur bristles in more ways than one. His full, neatly clipped moustache has military echoes from British Empire days, and yet his sense of discipline and formality frequently deserts him when he lets his fists fly. In terms of style, Arthur's choice of moustache is midway between the chevron – which is shaped towards the corners of the mouth but trimmed above the lip – and the more imposing walrus that spills over the edges.

While Arthur's moustache is a vital part of his appearance, it's also somewhat out of keeping with the times. As a fashionable facial feature, it had in fact begun to fall out of favour before the turn of the century. Then came the outbreak of the First World War, when men found more pressing and practical reasons to reach for the razor. In the trenches, where troops were required to snap on gas masks as if their lives depended on it, a soldier with any kind of facial hair risked compromising the seal. Once a required feature for soldiers serving in the British Army, the moustache was only dropped as mandatory from the King's Regulations in 1916. It's no surprise to see that

Chief Inspector Campbell sports the kind of 'tache that might have caused a soldier problems on the frontline. Indeed, he is constantly needled by Tommy about the fact that his 'reserved occupation' meant he did not fight during the war.

By 1919, and especially through the 1920s, the clean-shaven look became an established one for men across all classes. Ultimately, while his brothers and baby-faced cousin, Michael, comply with the sleek, hairless and ultimately modern look of the times, Arthur Shelby is content for his old-school moustache to reflect his values as the Peaky Blinder who commands respect through discipline.

When it comes to bringing out the panache in his personality, Aberama Gold knows how to make his moustache do all the talking. He only chooses to grow it late in the 1920s, but the teased ends create a rakish impression that helps to earn Polly Gray's acceptance of his hand in marriage. It hints towards the Hungarian style, extending outwards from the centre, which is a reflection of Aberama's East European Gypsy roots.

Alfie Solomons' moustache is somewhat eclipsed by his magnificent beard. It's an expression of his Orthodox Jewish heritage as much as a statement of his status as a wise gangster who seeks to stay one step ahead of his rivals. Grand Duke Leon Petrovich Romanov's moustache is notable for framing his impressively extended and imperial goatee, with cheek and jawline hair clipped back to lengthen the shape of the face. On the other end of the moustache scale the fascist leader, Sir Oswald Mosley, sports a pencil-thin design. It's imposing, but clipped and trim, reflecting the personality of his *Peaky Blinders* character.

NARROWBOATS, BARGES AND CANALS

'Our dad's boat. The boat I was born on. We've never got off it ... We've never got off it and we never fucking will!'

Unusually for a city, Birmingham does not feature a major river flowing through it. Instead, a network of man-made waterways provided critical transportation links for industry and wider society, including underworld players seeking to move goods quietly – often under cover of moonlight.

The first canals were built in the 1750s. They marked the beginning of a rapid growth period for the construction of man-made waterways, which continued until the 1830s. With over four thousand miles of engineered waterways across the UK (with horse-drawn vessels before steam engines and then diesel motors took over), the canals were a critical cog in keeping the big wheel of the Industrial Revolution turning. Birmingham, in particular, boasted more miles of waterways than Venice. With factories, warehouses and accommodation for the workforce springing up along the banks, the canals helped to define the shape of communities in the city.

As a distribution network, Britain's waterways enjoyed a golden age of activity and importance until the middle of the nineteenth century. Then, railways began to offer a faster, efficient alternative for the movement of many goods – as did the push for modern road building.

By the time soldiers returned from the frontline after the First World War, the role of the canal as an

industrial artery was in decline. The waterways were
still in use, but mostly for the transportation of very
heavy loads such as iron and coal, or to keep costs down
if delivery time wasn't a pressing issue.

The fact that attention was turning to other forms of
transport might well have suited an old-school boat-
man like Peaky Blinder associate, Charlie Strong. With
most goods shipped from his yard covered by tarpaulin, for good reason, he could be more confident that
his activities wouldn't draw unwanted attention.
Charlie's fleet includes narrowboats with cabin quarters and open barges designed to accommodate heavy
goods – or for cushioning Danny Whizz-Bang's fall
after Tommy seemingly shoots him in the back of the
head in front of two Italians who wish to see him dead.
Both types of vessel are purpose-built to fit the
restricted width of the locks across Britain's canal
system, which are used to raise and lower boats to
differing stretches of water level.

It isn't just Charlie who has a strong connection to
the canals. Polly lost her husband in an accident that
saw him crushed between a vessel and the cut, and
Tommy himself was born on a barge. This was not
unusual at a time when members of marginalised travelling communities frequently lived on narrowboats.
In the late 1800s, as the waterways faced economic
decline due to rising competition from the railways
and roads, many itinerant boatmen faced hardship.
In order to keep afloat economically, some then
housed their families on the vessels they owned. It's an
experience that no doubt bonds Tommy to the canals.
Having been brutally beaten by Sabini and his men, he
even finds in a narrowboat a place of calm convales-
cence as Curly escorts him to a London meeting with

Alfie Solomons in order to plot his fight back. The fading role of the canal in Britain's industry stands in stark contrast to its importance to the Peaky Blinders – from smuggling goods to travelling incognito – in their rise to power.

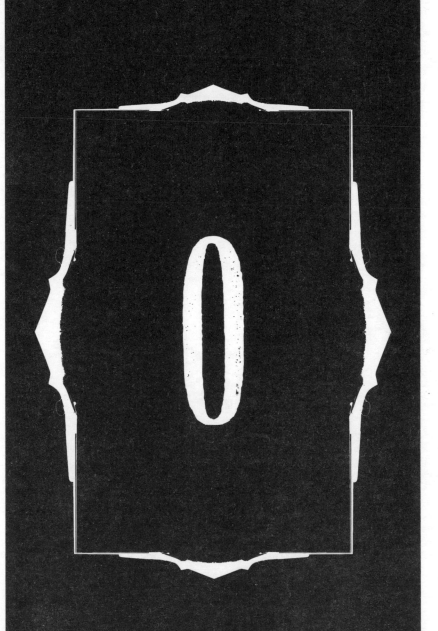

OPIUM

'No salt, no flour ... no lies.'

When Brilliant Chang presents the Peaky Blinders with an opportunity to help smuggle a consignment of 'the purest opium that has ever arrived in Europe' from London to the docks at Liverpool by barge, Tommy can call upon his experience as a user to know what he's dealing with. It's a drug he uses frequently as a means of escaping from his demons from the war, and one that had played both a colourful and insidious role in British life since the late 1700s.

Opium is the name given to a naturally occurring latex harvested from poppy pods. It contains a range of opiate substances with strong sedative properties. Opiates slow down body functions like heart rate and breathing, as well as reducing pain. Regular opium use can lead to physical and psychological dependency, and overdose can be fatal.

Despite the serious dangers presented by opium, which is now categorised as a Class A drug in the UK, there was a time before the Peaky Blinders when it was considered by the government to be a highly lucrative commodity on the international market.

Just over one hundred years before Brilliant Chang makes his proposition to Tommy Shelby, Britain was effectively the leading exporter of opium to China from India. There, the poppy grew in abundance. Such was the taxable profit to be made that it allowed the East India Company to thrive by selling the drug to Chinese merchants. When China placed restrictions on the trade in the middle of the nineteenth century, rightly concerned by the economic and social consequences, Britain even fought two opium wars with the country.

Eventually, with over 15 million opium users in the country, China fought back by legalising the drug, growing its own poppies and becoming the leading global exporter itself. By the time Tommy turns to smoking opium to deal with the horrors he'd witnessed in the tunnels and trenches on the Western Front during the First World War, China had become the primary supplier to Europe.

In Victorian times, opium was strongly associated with the expanding Chinese enclaves, such as Limehouse in London. Here, the demand largely came from merchant seamen who had become addicted to the drug on their travels to the Far East, but stories crept into the public domain of sinister and exotic dens wreathed in opium smoke.

Despite the stereotyping, opium was readily available to the British public in a legitimate form. Morphine, heroin and codeine are all synthesised from the opiates found in the drug, and in some forms were a popular medicine in the late nineteenth and early twentieth century. An opiate mixed with alcohol and herbs – laudanum – was a widely used 'tonic' through the nineteenth century and into the early decades of the next. Available from the chemist, it was used to treat a range of ailments, from sleeping difficulties to headaches, and even for babies as their milk teeth came through. In *Peaky Blinders*, Tommy swigs some from a small bottle 'to keep warm' while lost in thought in front of a campfire, and when the effects kick in it summons visions of his late wife, Grace. Polly Gray also produces a small vial when it matters most, as Linda Shelby writhes in pain having been shot in the arm at the climax of her stand-off with Arthur outside Arrow House.

It wasn't until the 1920s, as the dangers of opium and opiates became widely understood, that controls began to tighten. As for Tommy Shelby, his relationship with the drug takes place as social attitudes towards it were set to change significantly. For this Peaky Blinder, opium is both a personal medicine for dealing with his demons and a potential business opportunity in smuggling Chang's consignment to the USA that could make millions on the black market.

OVERCOAT

'No admission if you've any weapons!'

It's as iconic as the haircut, the boots, suit, shirt and the baker's boy cap. It's also sufficiently big and heavy to conceal a gun or a cosh, and a measure of a true Peaky Blinder. The overcoat of choice for Tommy and his brothers also looks as good today as it did one hundred years ago.

Tommy Shelby often wears a black, single-breasted, full-length overcoat made from heavy wool. The lining is a deep blood red, which provides a flash of colour as he marches on with his head down and cap worn low over his brow. Complete with wide peaked lapels, and broad shoulders, it has strong echoes of the military-issue trench coat worn by soldiers in the First World War.

Along with the tendency to hold on to their boots after demobilisation, many former soldiers also chose to keep their coats to wear on civvy street. These were hard-wearing garments designed to keep out the cold and biting winds, after all. Many also considered them to be a sign of patriotism and pride. As a reflection of his status as a man of influence across Small Heath, Tommy's overcoats are a cut above the rest. Tailored and imposing, whether crow black or dark blue – and often featuring a plush, velvet collar – such coats are a central part of his uniform.

Arthur, John and Michael are also fond of a dark, heavy overcoat, with differing styles of lapel to suit their taste. Arthur favours a wide peak that draws attention to his signature bow tie, John's lapels are notched as if carved by a knife, while cousin Michael's entire overcoat ominously echoes Tommy's in design.

Get the fit

It's an outer garment that doesn't just look good with a suit, waistcoat and penny-collared shirt. A well-fitted overcoat is a finishing touch that works with any outfit. It's warm, protects against the elements and deserves a place in every wardrobe. Here's how to make it work for you:

- The right length of an overcoat is a matter of personal choice. Much depends on your height and leg measurement. A full-length overcoat that falls below the knee-line can leave the wearer looking bogged down – and on the short side. As a rule, an overcoat that finishes above the knee will provide enough length to make a strong impression.
- Your overcoat is designed to be worn over layers of clothing. If you're buying off the peg, rather than having a coat tailor-made, it's always worth trying

one out for size before purchasing. It might seem generous in fitting, but all that changes when wearing a suit or even a thick jumper. An overcoat that feels like a squeeze isn't just uncomfortable to wear but also looks restricting. Stand tall, shoulders square, and let it breathe.

- When trying an overcoat for size, be sure to button up. Even if you intend to wear it loose, allowing the layers to come through and the back to flap as you walk, it's a useful measure. A good overcoat shouldn't be restricting, even with a full wardrobe on underneath. Nor should it be so loose that there's room at the front to conceal bricks of banknotes.

- In front of the mirror, note how the overcoat sits at the shoulder. The seam on each side should line up with the arms. If they don't make it out that far then the coat is too small and the sleeves will ride up too high when you're on the move. If the seams hang over the shoulders, it risks looking like the overcoat is wearing you.

- The arms of the overcoat should cover whatever you're wearing underneath. As a test, with your arms by your side, no jacket or jumper sleeve should be visible. Ideally, the sleeves of your overcoat should be in line with the top of your thumbs, and overlap any gloves you choose to wear.

PARLEY

'You don't parley when you're on the back foot.'

This is a word that's rarely heard today, but it's a vital negotiating tool for the Peaky Blinders when it comes to defusing conflicts and forming new allegiances.

Parley comes from the French verb *parler*, which means 'to speak'. In English, especially at the turn of the twentieth century, it was used to describe a discussion of some importance, or at a high level, often between parties who didn't see eye to eye.

Whether Tommy is meeting with Chief Inspector Campbell, the Lee family or any gangland kingpin who would gladly see him dead, through his eyes a parley is effectively a conversation with the potential for grave consequences. It's all the more reason why the Peaky Blinder never enters into one without being certain of the outcome first.

PEAKY BLINDERS

'This is the day we become respectable, but first we do the dirty work.'

The television series is the creation of screen writer Stephen Knight, and based on his parents' recollection of Birmingham in the early 1920s. In growing up, they remember vivid stories and snapshots of the street gang that inspired respect and also fear across Small Heath and beyond. Knight has always been clear in his belief that working-class history is often more

effectively handed down by stories through the generations than in history books. The resulting mythology
forms the starting point for his account of the life and
times of Tommy Shelby and the Peaky Blinders.

From what we know of the origins of the street gang
that inspired Knight's story, the real Peaky Blinders
date back to the last years of the 1800s. At a time of
hardship and deprivation, a number of largely young
men across the city organised and identified themselves as low-level criminal gangs on territorial lines.
While some believe that the term 'peaky blinder' was
used to describe anyone in Birmingham who operated
in a gang, the Small Heath group certainly claimed the
name with pride.

As a gang, Small Heath's Peaky Blinders were
involved in petty crime such as street robbery, theft
and burglary, as well as low-level racketeering. There
was no masterplan beyond making a living on the
margins and looking after their own.

Claiming Small Heath as their turf, it's believed the
district's Peaky Blinders frequently fought with rival
'slogging' gangs, which was a term that had come from
the boxing ring. Brawls were often brutal and bloody,
with gang members using blades and belts with heavy
buckles as weapons.

The Peaky Blinders formed allegiances and associa-
tions, just like the Shelbys and the Grays in Knight's
story. They simply didn't possess the same long-term
strategic thinking, daring and panache of Tommy and
his family to ascend to the same level of power. Even
so, as kings of the streets they identified themselves
with the same strong sense of style, making a powerful
and lasting impression with their dress sense.
Members wore sturdy boots, bell-bottomed trousers,

shirts with ties, silk scarves or even cravats, and, of course, the baker's boy cap. Debate continues as to whether the gang hid razors in the rim, or simply wore their caps low over the brow to avoid being identified. As for their hair, it's said that many favoured the same savage crops at the back and sides as the Shelbys, with the top worn longer and licked forward into what was sometimes known as a 'donkey fringe'. The wives and girlfriends of the gang members also took great care over their appearance. Colourful scarves, hats and jewellery were often the order of the day, along with the confidence to wear eye-catching and fequently expensive items, knowing nobody would dare rob them.

At the turn of the twentieth century – the high point of the gang's existence – names such as Ernest Bayles, Thomas Gilbert, Stephen McHickie and Harry Fowler were familiar to people across Small Heath, who preferred to stay on the side of the Peaky Blinders or simply steer clear. With a reputation as 'ruffians', they weren't a Robin Hood outfit that looked out for the disadvantaged, but one that largely thrived on intimidation and reputation.

The gang, however, went into decline in the early decades of the new century. A police crackdown overseen by a respected Chief Constable from Northern Ireland called Charles Rafter had a big impact on the activities of the slogging gangs – and the city's growing reputation for 'ruffianism'. At the same time, opportunities opened up in boxing clubs, association football teams and factory workplaces, which drew the next generation of potential gang members in different directions. Many would go on to join veteran Peaky Blinders in serving in the army during the First World War, and those who returned were older, battle-scarred and wiser.

Ironically – given his fate at the hands of Tommy Shelby in the series – it was Billy Kimber, who forced the Peaky Blinders to go to ground across Small Heath. With his business interests in racecourse protection rackets across the Midlands, Kimber and his Birmingham Boys had loftier ambitions than a Small Heath street gang, and were arguably better organised. As a result, they met with little resistance as they expanded their activities across the city.

By 1919, when Tommy Shelby begins to forge his reputation as an underworld boss in the television series, the real Peaky Blinders had all but disbanded. No doubt the principal players carried the gang's name and reputation with them, and remained known to the people of Small Heath, but a century would pass before the gang achieved worldwide recognition in the hands of a skilled screenwriter with family roots embedded in their world.

 ## PENNY CRUSH CINEMA

'You see, ladies, when you're out with a Blinder, you don't have to queue.'

Following the end of the First World War, the silver screen provided the first real opportunity for a mass audience to escape from the grind of everyday life, and it would continue to do so for much of the twentieth century. Purpose-built, independent cinemas, such as the Penny Crush in *Peaky Blinders*, offered the chance for an outing that was both affordable and rewarding on different levels. While 'talkies' didn't become a feature until the late 1920s, the opportunity to settle in front of a silent movie brought people flocking to the local picture houses early on.

Recently empowered by the efforts of the suffragettes, women in particular became enthusiastic cinemagoers. For Ada Shelby, it's a place for her to brood by herself over the family's hostility towards her relationship with communist sympathiser Freddie Thorne. She's aggrieved when Tommy uses his influence to stop the screening of a Rudolph Valentino movie and clear the seats so they can talk, while Arthur reacts violently when the police end his enjoyment of a movie in the company of two female friends.

In 1919, and through the Roaring Twenties, the popularity of cinemagoing in Britain continued to rise. It was a relatively new arrival in British life, with the first dedicated cinemas having only opened in the early years of that century. The introduction of fire regulations in 1909 largely informed the familiar shape of the Penny Crush Cinema and other movie theatres, with the projector (spooling highly flammable nitrate film stock) housed in a separate booth behind the auditorium.The seats were arranged on a slope so that everyone could view the screen, with aisles leading to the exits. Smoking was permitted, however, and auditoriums were notoriously choked when the lights went out and the projector coughed into life.

By the time Ada settles in for the opening credits, a picture house was commonplace in every major town and city across the country. Ornate plasterwork, vaulted ceilings with chandeliers and plush velvet seats encouraged a sense that a trip to the cinema was a special event, with many opening for matinee as well as evening screenings. Ticket prices varied, with cheap seats at the front – often just a row of wooden chairs or benches – then rising in price (as well as comfort) towards the back.

In some ways, the early picture houses, like the Penny Crush, became a victim of the rising popularity of cinemagoing. As demand exceeded capacity, and premises became crowded, smelly and worn out, many developed a reputation as 'flea pits'. Towards the end of the 1920s, film distribution networks came into play that often aligned with new, larger cinemas to show bigger box-office releases. For the independent picture house like Penny Crush, which had played such a central role in early post-war life, it would herald a more challenging market in which to survive. But for early patrons like Ada and Arthur, nothing could take away from the excitement and sense of occasion to be found in those formative days of British cinemagoing history.

POCKET SQUARE

'People look different at home ... off guard.'

In a dark, three-piece suit, Tommy Shelby sports one simple accessory that provides a flash of colour, class and confidence. The pocket square is a handkerchief folded deftly into the chest pocket of a suit jacket. It's largely there for decorative purposes, as opposed to being a handkerchief used to blow the nose, but though it's a small touch, it can speak volumes about the wearer's attention to detail.

Also sometimes called the pocket handkerchief, the pocket square dates back to Ancient Egypt, and has been a popular accessory for well-dressed gentlemen since the fifteenth century. Lace and silk were popular fabrics, and often embroidered in a display of wealth and taste. It's believed that early adopters from the upper classes dipped their squares in perfume as a means of combating the bad smells of the age.

As well as providing a scented distraction, which some believed would ward off illness, the pocket square was largely used for attending to the nose and face. Typically kept out of sight in the trouser pocket in the early years, it only migrated to the chest pocket in the nineteenth century. This was largely down to the fact that men carried coins in their trousers, and in an industrial age the handkerchief quickly got dirty. At the same time, the suit was becoming popular. By moving the pocket square onto display, men considered it to be a simple, cheap way to upgrade their wardrobe that added a dash of colour and individuality. Inevitably, after reaching for the square to catch a sneeze or dab the mouth, users would often stuff it into a spare pocket just to keep it out of sight. As a result, many men began to carry a separate handkerchief for hygiene purposes, reserving the pocket square solely for decoration.

By the 1920s, when Tommy and his associates are rarely seen without one, the silk or linen pocket square was considered to be the height of fashion. Part of the art of wearing a square with panache comes down to how the material was folded. With only the top section visible, a variety of methods have been practised to produce different looks. A triangle or points fold, for example, makes a virtue of one to four corners, while more ornate folds can transform a pocket square into the shape of a rose head.

Preferring to keep things simple, Tommy favours the Flat Fold (also known as the Presidential Fold). This reveals a neat band that potentially affords a striking contrast with the suit. It's also low maintenance, requiring little adjustment through the day.

The Flat Fold

- Lay your pocket square flat in front of you.
- Fold one side into the centre line.
- Fold the other side fully across.
- Repeat from the opposite side, so the handkerchief is approximately the same width as the chest pocket.
- Fold in half vertically, and then again, until you're left with a square.
- Choosing either a folded edge or rolled side to be visible, insert into the pocket.

Today, the pocket square is considered to be a perfectly acceptable suit accessory, and can be worn with or without a tie. It may not be commonplace, but there's no doubt it commands attention just as effectively as it did one hundred years ago.

 # POCKET WATCH

'Sadly, sometimes it's too late. And that's the thing about time. We can't get it back.'

For the Peaky Blinders, the pocket watch is a finishing touch that adds an air of prestige and precision-tooled glamour to any outfit. A glint of the chain that anchors the timepiece to the shirt or waistcoat is often all that's visible. Just like the glimpse of a gun holster under a jacket, it's enough to reveal that the wearer is someone with purpose who conceals more than first meets the eye.

The pocket watch was first produced in the sixteenth century. Early incarnations were cumbersome, boxy items that showed just the hour hand and even then barely kept the right time. It took one hundred years of design evolution before people stopped wearing the watch as a pendant around the neck. Instead, the time-piece was equipped with a chain and hoop that could be fastened through a button hole in the front of the wear-er's clothing. This allowed the watch to be dropped into a pocket, which became a lasting convention. Even then, it wasn't until the middle of the nineteenth century that the watch became the compact timepiece that could sit comfortably in the palm of a hand.

As the business of watchmaking advanced, moving away from the need for a key to wind up the device to a round knob or crown on the side instead, so the time-pieces produced became more affordable but by no means cheap. By the early decades of the twentieth century, as the Shelbys made their name, the smooth, pebble-shaped pocket watch was a sign of success or upward mobility. Like today's mobile phone, it reflected the wearer's status and personality. The pocket watch was also considered to be an heirloom. Sometimes featuring a personalised engraving on the back, it was a timepiece that could be passed down through the generations no matter what the monetary value.

Pocket watches increasingly varied in price, with the watch case fashioned from brass to gold. As glass fronts were a feature, many added protective hinged covers that could be flipped open with the deft use of a thumb. The watch chain also became a decorative item. The most popular kind was called the single Albert chain – after Prince Albert – which featured a T-bar at one end that could be fastened through a buttonhole. The Double Albert was for the more ostentatious, with the bar affixed to the chain in such a way that an eye-catching fob could be attached to the free end, a compass, fountain pen or even a cigarette case.

By 1919, the pocket watch was encountering some competition. Wristwatches had been in existence for centuries, but were considered to be a curiosity and also exclusively feminine devices. Attitudes changed during the First World War, when officers found it more efficient to check the time by peeking under their sleeve rather than fumbling in a pocket.

Despite the growing appeal of the wristwatch, the pocket watch endured until the early 1960s as a classic accessory for the modern man. During the 1920s, at the height of the Jazz era, the fashion-conscious secured their watches with long spring-ring chains attached to a belt loop. The timepiece itself was stowed in the trouser pocket, which led to the addition of an inner pocket, or 'watch pocket', to some garments; a feature later standardised by jeans manufacturers and commonly used for keys, spare change or condoms. As for the spring-ring chain, after the pocket watch fell out of fashion it was adopted by bikers as a means to secure their wallets in their back pockets while on the move, and later by the punk movement as a statement in its own right.

Even though society moved on from it in the middle of the twentieth century, the pocket watch had enjoyed four hundred years as the timepiece of choice. Such longevity can only give it a classic quality that still works well with a three-piece suit to this day. Whatever model or fastening, whether it's vintage or contemporary, the pocket watch is guaranteed to invest the same touch of class and assurance shown by Tommy Shelby and his associates a century earlier.

PRISON

'Do I look all right? This place is full of Sabini's men and fucking rats.'

For any crime family, prison is just one wrong move away in terms of strategy. Tommy Shelby will always seek to turn that to his advantage, but ultimately the Peaky Blinders are not above the law.

Throughout the story, several characters spend time inside. When it comes to crimes committed in the city and surrounding areas, the perpetrators end up behind bars at Birmingham's Winson Green Prison. It's here that the Digbeth Kid is brutally murdered by inmates aligned to Charles 'Darby' Sabini. Michael spends a short spell in solitary confinement in the same place, following his arrest for suspicion of arson by Chief Inspector Campbell, only to languish in the cells several years later along with Arthur and John charged with murder and sedition. It's a sentence set for a bleak ending when the trio are summoned to the gallows, while Polly faces the same fate in the women's wing. Tommy orchestrates a Royal Pardon with seconds to spare, but his family are quite clearly scarred by their experience inside the jailhouse walls.

Winson Green was the name of a Victorian-era prison located to the north-west of Birmingham's city centre, which now operates as HMP Birmingham. Its former frontage resembled castle ramparts, and became a familiar and forbidding landmark. As well as housing inmates, Winson Green carried out many executions until capital punishment was outlawed in the 1960s.

There's no doubt that Arthur, John, Michael and Polly suffered a traumatising climax to their time in jail in 1924. It would have come as little comfort to Arthur, John, Michael and Polly, but the fact is that conditions inside Britain's prisons had significantly improved just two years earlier. Up until 1922, prisoners were likely to have been kept in solitary, unheated cells. Indeed, Arthur would have experienced this for himself in 1921, having been held on remand in London after Alfie Solomons framed him for the killing of Billy Kitchen. Back then, as Arthur complained to John, who visited to find his older brother in shackles, vermin were a problem along with gang rivalry.

Following the 1922 reforms, prisoners were permitted to wear their own clothes, the food improved, and the concept of rehabilitating inmates through training and education courses was introduced. The eldest Shelby brother even appears relaxed when the officers unlock his cell door, stirring him from sleep. Then it dawns on him with horror that their trial has been brought forward, conducted in their absence, and the judge has sentenced them to hang.

PROHIBITION

'Tell your people in Chicago that Michael Gray will sign the import licence to New York. Three hundred barrels of English dry gin a month.'

Smuggling large quantities of alcohol across the Atlantic is a risky business, even if it does form part of Tommy's plan to outmanoeuvre the murderous New York Mafia wise guy, Luca Changretta. During the 1920s, however, at the height of America's Prohibition era, the rewards were immense, and could make it all worthwhile.

From 1920 to 1933, alcohol was outlawed in America. The production, transportation, distribution and sale of intoxicating liquor were classed as offences punishable by fines and even jail sentences. Due to a loophole in the law, the act of consuming alcohol was not banned. As a result, drinking went underground and into the control of a thriving black market.

Prohibition, which means the act of stopping something by law, was driven by a deep-seated fear among America's religious and social moralists that drinking was undermining society. Saloon bar culture was the main focus for concern, which was undeniably rowdy and often violent. The Temperance Movement led the charge, which gathered momentum through the late 1800s. Calls progressed from advocating moderation to outright teetotalism, which led to the gradual demonisation of alcohol. It was blamed for the breakdown of families and moral values, and debauchery at every level, as well as accidents in a predominantly industrial workplace. By the turn of the century, temperance societies existed in almost every state across the country.

Support for an outright ban on alcohol was driven by the influential evangelical Protestant church and a strong women's movement – which believed alcohol was a destructive influence on marriage. Industrialists and factory owners, seeking to improve productivity, added their voices, until finally the call for Prohibition was recognised at a political level. In 1918, an amendment was added to the American Constitution. This brought a law into force that marked the beginning of an era that had unexpected consequences for the nation. Not only did the outlawing of the manufacture, distribution and sale of alcohol fail to quell America's thirst; it also created an opportunity for the Mafia and a global network of criminal enterprises to meet demand.

As Tommy Shelby is well aware, it was Chicago kingpin, Al Capone, who became the most influential figure in the covert importation of alcohol into America. Through the early years of the 1920s, Capone established rum-smuggling lines from the Caribbean and dispatched men over the border into Canada to hijack whiskey consignments by road and rail. Other Mafia bosses such as Lucky Luciano in New York also got in on the act, which led to an increase in cooperation between crime families, but also violence. In backrooms and basements, people began to set up homemade stills to make 'bootleg' alcohol, 'moonshine' or 'bathtub gin', along with more ambitious alcohol production ventures overseen by The Mob. In cities across the country, secret drinking establishments known as 'speakeasies' opened for business. This coincided with the growing popularity for jazz through the 1920s and the post-war desire to party and live the high life. This heady mix proved so intoxicating that the underground culture for booze simply exploded. Despite the recruitment of Prohibition agents to stamp out illegal activity, this proved impossible to police. Many agents were bribed or intimidated by the Mafia, and for every speakeasy or still that was raided, several more would open up.

In underworld Britain, the opportunity to supply America's demand for alcohol proved impossible to ignore. Smuggling spirits such as whiskey – both Irish and Scottish varieties – by ships became big business, using transatlantic trade routes. In *Peaky Blinders*, this is capitalised upon by both Alfie Solomons and the Peaky Blinders. When Tommy Shelby first takes the narrowboat to Camden Docks, the Jewish gangster shows him round his 'bakery', which is quite clearly in the business of making and crating bootleg rum bound for America. Tommy himself tries his hand at production, refining a gin based on his father's recipe 'for the eradication of seemingly incurable sadness'. His large, elaborate gin still, with equipment and bottles filling a back room behind Charlie Strong's yard, is an example of the extent that bootleggers would go to serve a market across the Atlantic that had only come into existence through government controls. For the Peaky Blinders, having secured a supply line to Chicago, the potential reward vastly outweighed the risks.

If Prohibition aimed to create a sober nation, the legislation simply highlighted how entrenched drinking had become in society. Towards the late

1920s, it was evident that banning alcohol merely empowered criminal enterprise. It had led to jails filling with people who would otherwise have been law-abiding citizens, while an unregulated industry meant that bootleggers were sometimes producing alcohol at dangerous strengths per volume and even batches that could kill. Slowly but steadily, voices started to demand that the amendment be repealed. This gathered volume following the 1929 stock market crash and the Great Depression that began to loom. With the economy tanking, and only the underworld kingpins like Capone profiting from the situation – often with violent results – it was widely recognised that a legitimate alcohol industry could make a valuable contribution to the nation's recovery. Back under government control, it would bring in tax, create jobs and ultimately cut out the criminal element.

In 1932, Franklin D. Roosevelt ran for the White House promising to end Prohibition, beating the incumbent President Hoover by a landslide. One year later, for the first time in America's history, an amendment to America's Constitution was repealed. It is believed that Roosevelt himself marked the end of an era now regarded as a failure in social intervention by declaring, 'what America needs now is a drink'.

PROSTITUTION

'The lodgings the police department picked for you . . . the landlady used to run the most famous whorehouse in Stretchford. She's only semi-retired.'

Tommy's words of warning for Major Campbell are met at first with indignation, but it isn't long before the latter avails himself of Mrs Ross's services. In 1920s Britain, at a time of economic struggle, prostitution was a necessary means for some women to make ends meet. Living in poverty, often with children to feed, the oldest profession became the only means for some to survive.

Before she joins the Shelby family business as a secretary, and then ultimately becomes Tommy's wife, Lizzie Stark relies on prostitution in order to provide for her young family. Following the end of the First World War, in which many women were widowed and left in great financial hardship, some were left with little choice but to sell their bodies. It placed them at great risk of violence and robbery, not least at the hands of pimps. Across the social spectrum, prostitution in early post-war Britain was only thinly hidden from view. As well as working on the streets and from private addresses, women were drawn into brothels like the outfit run by Mr Zhang alongside his dry-cleaning business. It's one visited by Campbell himself; supposedly an upholder of the law, but someone prepared to turn a blind eye to satisfy his own needs.

Attitudes towards prostitution, somewhat typified by Campbell, were largely intact from Victorian times. Morally, the practice was denounced by the Church and upright members of society, and, legally, prostitutes faced conviction under solicitation laws. Meanwhile, men who purchased sex went unpunished. Women like Lizzie were considered to be 'fallen', and beyond help, and indeed when John declares that he is set to make an honest woman of her, the family respond to him with incredulity. Tommy himself is one of Lizzie's regular clients until an emotional relationship emerges to blur the boundaries.

As Lizzie seeks to put her past behind her, in the wake of the Suffrage Movement women's groups began to challenge the legal framework around prostitution. In particular, concern focused on the fact that successful prosecution for solicitation was often based on little (but required) supporting evidence from arresting officers. If a woman was found guilty, even without proof that she was actively offering her services, she was legally categorised as a 'common prostitute'.

Through the 1920s, critics argued that the stigma carried by such an offensive term was ruinous for convicted women who already faced enough challenges in life. It could lead to future police harassment and a social stigma that was near impossible to shake off. Following mounting pressure, in 1928 the government commissioned a review into prostitution laws. The findings, published the following year, were considered to be a whitewash, with no statute change to the 'common prostitute' categorisation. It also disappointed those who wanted the law to recognise the many women in the sex industry as victims. Nevertheless, by highlighting their plight, including the dangers they faced, the review introduced into public debate some searching questions about the men who created demand for the trade.

Arrest rates for solicitation dropped throughout the 1930s. This was largely down to the criticism directed at the police and courts for convicting without sufficient evidence. The laws would not be revisited in the UK again until the 1950s, and it wasn't until a 2007 review that the term 'common prostitute' was subsequently dropped as a legal classification.

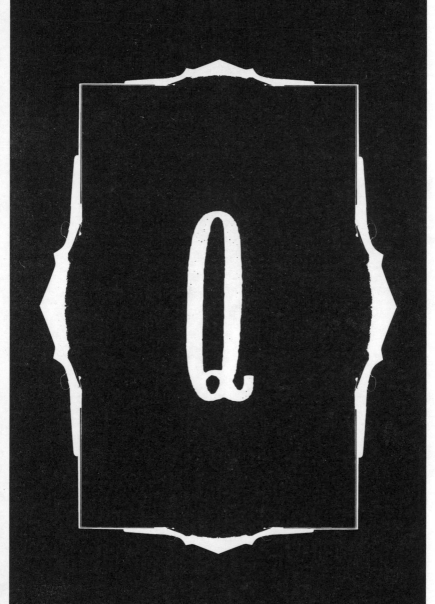

QUEENSBERRY RULES

'Come on, Gypsy Boy, let's go!'

When Bonnie Gold springs from his corner to face Alfie Solomons' fighter, Goliath, he's confident he can legitimately take down his opponent in the fourth round. The hall in which the Peaky Blinders have staged the match is rammed to the rafters, and bets have been laid on the outcome. Despite the fact that the event is hosted and promoted by a criminal gang, the fight itself is conducted under a recognised code of conduct established just over fifty years earlier to prevent a bloody brawl.

By the early nineteenth century, prizefighting was a popular pastime. It was also unregulated, operating under loose rules from the 1740s with impromptu bare-knuckle fights staged with indeterminate numbers of rounds, and an attitude that whatever it took to win was acceptable. The resulting bouts could be rowdy affairs that often led to grievous injuries. In response, from the 1830s, many contests were conducted under the London Prize Ring rules. The guidelines forbade, for example, kicking, head-butting and eye-gouging, but did little to protect fighters in other respects.

According to London Prize Ring rules, rounds were determined by a fighter hitting the ground, after which he was given thirty seconds to 'come to scratch' for the next round. If a fighter failed to stay in contention, often because he was badly beaten or unconscious, his opponent was declared the winner. While the rules provided some structure and parameters to a fight, it still remained a brutal experience that was determined by the last man standing. With violence frequently spilling over into the crowds, prizefighting was largely considered to be the preserve of the lower classes.

In a bid to broaden appeal to the upper classes, and encourage boxing to be recognised as a sport, many felt that the savagery on display could be tamed through further discipline. In 1865, a Welshman called John Graham Chambers of the Amateur Athletic Club began work on a new set of rules. He proposed that – in contrast to the London Prize Ring rules – rounds should be strictly limited to three minutes of fighting followed by one minute of rest. Crucially, Chambers introduced the concept that padded gloves should be mandatory.

Drawing up twelve rules in total, and aware that he needed some kind of influential seal of approval, Chambers sought the patronage of John Sholto Douglas, the 9th Marquis of Queensberry. On their publication in 1867, the Queensberry Rules were at first dismissed by the old guard in boxing circles as being too soft. It was the younger generation of boxers, however, who saw the potential in the Queensberry approach to allow a certain pugilistic craft to thrive while upholding notions of sportsmanship and fair play.

Coupled with the introduction of weight divisions, the Queensberry Rules gradually took over from the London Prize Club Rules. As the new regulations were adopted in boxing clubs and competitions over the decades that followed, the transition period was still marked with some ferocity in the ring by boxers schooled in bare-knuckle fighting. Boxing without gloves continued in some quarters long into the twentieth century, notably among Gypsy brawlers, and indeed when Arthur Shelby Snr first makes an appearance, he's in the ring under the old rules.

By contrast, young Bonnie Gold recognises that if he is going to make his name as a professional boxer, he needs to adhere to the Queensberry Rules. By the 1920s, following a world war in which the military had adopted boxing as a training aid, this was no longer seen as a soft option but as a means of developing skill, agility and character. Indeed, the talented young fighter has the backing and encouragement of both Tommy and Arthur, both raised in an era when John Graham Chamber's regulations had become an established feature in the ring, and had laid the foundation for the sport of modern boxing around the world.

The Queensberry Rules

- It must be a fair match in a twenty-four-foot ring or smaller if not practical.
- No wrestling moves are permitted.
- All rounds must be three minutes long with a one-minute rest in between.
- If a boxer goes down, he must get up without help before the referee reaches the count of ten. The boxer standing must remain in the neutral corner.
- If a boxer is hanging on to the ropes in a helpless state, it will be counted as a knockdown.
- Only the boxers and referee can be in the ring during a round.
- If a fight has to be stopped due to any outside interference, the referee must name a place and time to finish the fight. Alternatively, both boxers can agree to call the fight a draw.

- Gloves must be a fair size, and also new or of very good quality.
- If a glove bursts or comes off, then it must be replaced to the satisfaction of the referee.
- If a boxer drops to one knee, it is counted as a knock-down, and if he is struck while down in this position, he is entitled to the stakes.
- No footwear with spikes or springs can be worn.
- In all other respects, the fight should be conducted under London Prize Ring rules.

RAZOR BLADE

'I swear I will cut you open.'

In *Peaky Blinders*, the safety blade designed for shaving without causing nicks or cuts takes on a whole new purpose when stitched into the brow of the gang's baker boy caps. For Tommy, Arthur, John and Finn, it's a weapon within easy reach that can be used in fights to slash their victims across the face or brow, blinding them with blood. Even Polly is not afraid to wield a blade, as she threatens Esme one time for prying into her affairs.

The concept of a blade with a protective edge had been in existence since the late 1800s, but it was a travelling salesman by the name of King Camp Gillette who was responsible for the mass-market, disposable blade that dominated the twentieth century. Working alongside a machinist called William Emery Nickerson, it took several years for them to develop the blade, stamped from a carbon sheet so that it was sufficiently sharp. In 1903, having patented the design – which was mounted on a frame and handle and then simply replaced when the blades wore out – the fledgling Gillette company launched the disposable razor. The product become so popular that Gillette supplied American troops during the First World War, before expanding to dominate the European market through the 1920s.

In the hands of Tommy Shelby and his brothers in *Peaky Blinders*, the blade serves as a formidable weapon. It's certainly become a feature of the mythology surrounding the Birmingham street gangs that inspired the story, even though they were believed to be on the wane when use of the safety blade became widespread across Britain.

In the early decades of the 1900s, and for the century preceding it, men relied on the straight razor for shaving, and often left that task to the steady hand of the barber. A long blade that folded into a handle, the device offered no protective guard, unlike the safety razor and the disposable variety that followed. Also known as the cut-throat razor for good reason, it became the weapon of choice, most notoriously for several criminal groups in Glasgow through the 1920s and 30s, including the Billy Boys, who were known as a 'razor gang'. Carrying a straight blade wasn't exclusive to gangs north of the border in postwar Britain. Acts of violence involving men working for Charles 'Darby' Sabini and Alf Solomon frequently involved razors as much as coshes and guns.

THE RITZ

'*In future I shall be dining here quite a bit.*'

Money talks to the *maître d'* when Tommy produces a roll of banknotes and places it on the hotel's front desk. After initially receiving a frosty welcome – having identified himself as a dining companion of the hotel's bill-dodging guest, Grand Duke Leon Petrovich Romanov – the Peaky Blinder is ushered in with all the grace and cordiality associated with a hotel of this calibre. For this is The Ritz; a world-famous name by today's standards, but one that had only begun to

214

establish its reputation when Tommy Shelby makes his way to the dining rooms.

A grade-II-listed building and a five-star hotel, The Ritz, London, was opened in 1906 by Swiss hotelier César Ritz. A former manager of The Savoy – yet another prestigious hotel in the capital – Ritz was a business associate of the legendary chef and father of modern French cooking, Auguste Escoffier. The Piccadilly-based hotel would be the second to bear his name, following the establishment of the Hôtel Ritz Paris in 1898. Ritz had forged a reputation for attention to detail and elegance, and the concept that 'the customer is always right'. In opening a hotel in London, he intended to cater for a high society familiar with elite country clubs. By the time Tommy makes his entrance in 1924, however, the hotel had only just established the profile and reputation it enjoys to this day.

Despite being slow to attract the anticipated level of custom in the early years following the hotel's opening, fortunes changed for The Ritz, London, after PM David Lloyd George began to use the address for strategy meetings during the First World War. Business picked up considerably after 1918, as politicians, wealthy industrialists and socialites came to believe that the hotel's luxurious surroundings and impeccable service made it the place to be seen in.

Throughout the 1920s, The Ritz strengthened its reputation as a luxury hotel. Regular diners and guests included Edward, Prince of Wales and future King of England before his abdication, the Hollywood actresses Rita Hayworth and Tallulah Bankhead, and the playwright Noel Coward. During his legendary 1921 return to Britain from America, where he had established himself as one of the most recognisable film stars in the world, Charlie Chaplin chose to stay at The Ritz. Vast crowds formed outside, hoping for a glimpse of the movie star. Chaplin stayed in the Regal Suite on the first floor. With the street packed below, he famously ventured out onto the balcony to throw white carnations to his fans. To commemorate his stay, The Ritz would go on to name a suite after him.

Tommy Shelby is not the only Peaky Blinder to enjoy the opulent and lavish experience offered by the hotel. On her return from America for fertility treatment – with a first husband who would eventually take his own life – Grace Burgess calls Tommy from her room in The Ritz and arranges to meet him at Ada's townhouse.

Throughout the 1930s and after the Second World War, the hotel would continue to build on its reputation, hosting high-profile guests from Sir Winston Churchill to the oil tycoon John Paul Getty III – who had a residency there – Jackie Onassis and the Queen Mother. For Tommy Shelby, sitting calmly opposite the Russian exile as he devours fine caviar as if it might be his last opportunity, the magnificent dining room at The Ritz is just another place in which to do business in order to expand the Shelby empire.

RUM

'The problem, right, between rum and gin, is that gin, right, it leads to the melancholy, whereas rum incites violence. It also allows you to be liberated from your self-doubt.'

Alfie Solomons is a man who knows a thing or two about rum. From his Camden bakery, which is all but a front, he distils, bottles and smuggles cases of a spirit with a long and challenging history that entwines Britain with the Caribbean.

By the early 1900s, almost three hundred years since the British Navy captured Barbados, St Kitts and Jamaica and one hundred years since the abolition of the slave trade that followed, rum had become a commodity that continued to flow. Introduced to the UK by homecoming sailors, this strong, spiced and sweet alcohol quickly found a place alongside the British taste for gin and whiskey.

Rum is made from distilled sugar-cane juice or molasses. As sugar isn't a crop that's easily grown in the northern hemisphere, rum importation into the UK became big business. Companies established ware-houses on the banks of the Thames to age and blend different grades and varieties of the spirit for a grow-ing, thirsty market.

For an underground distiller like Alfie Solomons, illegally producing rum on British soil would have been both a challenge and a fine art. A bootlegger at the time would know how to distil a low-quality rum using sugar-cane syrup, which became a popular commercial product in the twentieth century, but the purist would always go the distance by sourcing molasses. Whatever Alfie's methods, he's clearly established a recipe for success in supplying a black-market demand in Prohibition America through the 1920s.

CHARLES 'DARBY' SABINI

'Alfie, we've been fighting each other since we were at school. And also we've been friends. It goes back and forwards. How much better is it when we're friends?'

Charles 'Darby' Sabini is in hostile territory. He's facing the Jewish gang leader in the bowels of his Camden bakery, and appealing to their shared history in a bid to stop the Peaky Blinders from moving in on the capital. Sabini agrees a fragile pact with Alfie Solomons, and Tommy Shelby must play one off against the other in order to survive.

In real life, the two figures behind the characters of Sabini and Solomons in the series did indeed share a classroom. As well as briefly attending the same school, both came from immigrant backgrounds, and possessed a strong sense of identity as they forged their reputations as lords of the underworld in post-war London.

Octavius Sabini was born in Holborn in 1888 to an English mother and Italian father. Popular with Italian immigrants, the area was known as Little Italy, and though Sabini considered himself to be an Englishman, his Mediterranean heritage would have been a strong influence on his upbringing. Sabini was known by several names, often introducing himself as Charles and also 'Darby', which was a nickname that would also become central to his identity.

Sabini attended a school for delinquent children, which may have been down to his known flair as a pick-pocket, before leaving education at thirteen to work for a boxing promoter. He proved to be a promising young fighter, possessing an imposing build and reach, but a lack of commitment saw him step away from the ring to take up security work as a bouncer. In his twenties, Charles 'Darby' Sabini had earned a reputation in Holborn and surrounding areas as an uncompromising brawler and enforcer who was unafraid to get physical as a means of settling disputes. At the same time, he became involved in both gang life and racecourse betting. The combination led him to establish a shake-down racket by skimming a percentage of the takings from bookmakers to 'protect' their stands.

Sabini opened several nightclubs, including The Eden. He could count on more than a hundred foot-soldiers, as well as connections in the police that once got him off a charge of shooting a gun at a racetrack, to stamp his authority as a gangland boss with serious influence. At the very height of his power, with far-reaching interests in theft and gambling, he was regarded as the most powerful gangster in southern England.

In contrast to the sharp dress sense of his *Peaky Blinders* character, Sabini was said to favour the collarless shirt and cap of the working class. A married man with children, he earned a reputation for being courteous, kind and charitable. At the same time, he was regarded by rival gangs as a formidable crime boss. Before the Racecourse Wars of 1921, which saw gangs go head to head for control of the bookmakers' pitches across the south of England, it's believed he was on cordial terms with Billy Kimber from Birmingham. When the two sides came to blows over business, resulting in several ugly razor fights, Sabini persuaded his old schoolfriend, Alf Solomon, to align his Jewish gang against the mob from the Midlands.

The dispute with Billy Kimber came to a head in March of that year, when Sabini arranged talks with his rival at his house in Kings Cross. It was a gangland summit that would culminate in a mysterious shooting on the street outside, leaving Kimber seriously wounded and Alf Solomon in court charged with unlawful wounding. At trial, Kimber declined to point the finger at Solomon – quite possibly to protect any negotiations with Sabini – who was found not guilty and released.

Throughout the 1920s, by forming unlikely allegiances with Solomon and other criminal players while also seeking an air of legitimacy by dealing with the Jockey Association, Charles 'Darby' Sabini gained the upper hand against the Birmingham mobster. Tightening control of pitches across the south of England, and forcing Kimber to downsize his expansion plans from the north, he became known as 'King of the Racehorse Gangs'. By the end of the decade, however, efforts by the Jockey Club and the police to completely rid the racecourses of criminality effectively squeezed out Sabini altogether. Moving to the East Sussex coast, he turned his attention to greyhound racing, along with gambling and drinking clubs in the 1930s, only for global events to overtake his fortunes with the outbreak of the Second World War.

Despite being born and bred in England, Sabini's Italian heritage led to his arrest and interment in 1941 as a potential enemy of the state. Shortly afterwards, under investigation by the authorities, he was charged with handling stolen goods and spent the duration of the war in prison. His only son, serving in the RAF, was killed in action over Egypt. Grieving behind bars,

Sabini could do nothing but watch in resignation as rivals picked his criminal empire to the bone.

Following the war, with his underworld business all but gone, Sabini retired to a villa on the coast at Hove. He spent his last years relatively quietly, and with little evidence of the fortune he had amassed, dying in 1950 aged sixty-two. As well as being immortalised as a leading underworld character in *Peaky Blinders*, Charles 'Darby' Sabini is said to have been the inspiration for the underworld kingpin, Colleoni, in Graham Greene's classic 1938 novel, *Brighton Rock*.

SANDWICH

'The single stroke of mustard is the thing. The fine detail.'

When Chief Inspector Campbell waxes lyrical to Moss about the finish to his tongue-and-pickle sandwich, he could be talking about a work of fine craftsmanship. A man who likes things done properly, Campbell would appreciate the combination of flavours at a time when food had a tendency to be stodgy and plain.

Through the early decades of the twentieth century, the sandwich underwent a quiet revolution. The art of placing a filling between two slices of bread wasn't new, having been in existence by then for two hundred years. Initially, the sandwich was enjoyed by the upper classes, but industrialisation and a hungry workforce soon saw its popularity spread. By the turn of the twentieth century, it had transcended class to become the true food of the people. Portable and tasty, it found a place from formal high tea on a country lawn to a snatched lunchbreak beside the glare of a factory furnace, or a shared bite to eat between an officer of the law, who has pledged to take down the Peaky Blinders and his subordinate, who is also secretly on their payroll.

Campbell isn't the only character in *Peaky Blinders* to enjoy a sandwich. Polly Gray prepares some with great reverence for her son Michael, while Derby Sabini tries not to make a mess of his suit while eating a doorstep-cut sandwich on a chair in a blood-stained boxing ring. Things became considerably easier for the likes of the London crime lord when sliced bread came on the market in the 1930s. From that moment on, the sandwich was here to stay.

The choice of filling one hundred years ago may not compare with that of today, nor the variety of bread used to make it. Tastes evolve, of course, and some once-popular choices have been left behind. Here are several sandwich varieties that pack an authentic *Peaky Blinders* bite:

Tongue and pickle

The cut of beef from the tongue of the cow might not be in popular demand today, but in the early twentieth century it was considered to be an affordable and tasty treat. A high-fat cut that responds well to slow cooking, it can be roasted, boiled, baked or grilled, and then sliced thinly for a sandwich.

Ham and cress

It's a filling that has withstood the test of time, though cress has slipped from the sandwich menu in recent years to be replaced by cheese. In the 1920s, when landlady and semi-retired prostitute Mrs Ross offers ham and cress as a choice to her new lodger, Chief Inspector Campbell, this commonplace, peppery herb was a common sandwich feature. Quick and easy to grow in a British climate, and rich in vitamins, it served as a cheap and nutritious seasoning.

Shrimp paste

When Polly Gray prepares Michael for his first day out with his cousins, she packs him off with dainty sandwiches. When he unwraps them en route, Arthur looks on in disbelief. It's not the sandwich or the filling that surprises him, but the fact that his young cousin would need anything other than whiskey to keep him afloat through the day. Shrimp paste was commonplace in sandwiches in the early twentieth century. Comprising boiled and chopped or pounded shrimp in butter with seasoning and sometimes lemon, it's still available off the shelf today.

SHELL-SHOCK

'Danny, you're home! We're all home in England! You're not in France. You're not an artillery shell, Danny. You're a man!'

Pinning their former brother in arms to the floor of the Garrison, Tommy and Freddie Thorne know exactly what's caused Danny Whizz-Bang to crash in the grip of an intense, hallucinatory panic attack. Much as with Barney Thompson, another army comrade in need of care and understanding, Danny's wartime experience has left him a ghost of his former self.

Early in the war, many soldiers were evacuated from the frontline suffering from a range of troubling symptoms. Sufferers would experience anything from uncontrollable fear and panic to insomnia, memory loss, confusion, hallucinations, and even impaired speech, sight and movement.

At first, doctors were mystified. While the condition was dismissed in some quarters as a sign that a sufferer didn't possess the necessary qualities for battle – and in some cases classed as cowardice – medical experts explored the possibility that it was caused by a form of brain damage. Even when sufferers had no head wound, focus remained on the possibility that exposure to detonating shells had resulted in a blast injury inside the skull.

In 1915, an army medical officer called Charles Myers proposed the term 'shell-shock'. Alongside the prevailing attitude that some kind of blast-related concussion was the cause, he introduced the concept that soldiers were suffering from psychological issues as a result of a traumatic experience. By 1917, support for both explanations led to a military request that frontline medics cease using the blanket term 'shell-shock' in favour of 'Not Yet Diagnosed (Nervous)'. Sufferers were then examined away from battle to determine if the injury was physical ('shell-shock: wound') or psychological ('shell-shock: sick'), and then subsequently assessed for fitness. If the soldier was deemed unable to fight due to a physical head injury, then he would be eligible for an honourable discharge and war pension. Should he be diagnosed with an 'affliction of the nerves', however, no such option was available. Instead, after a period of rest there was every chance he would be returned to battle.

By the time hostilities ended, it was widely known that the majority of those soldiers suffering from shell-shock presented no physical head injuries. By now, thousands of veterans were struggling to reintegrate with society (from the rank-and-file foot-soldiers to officers), with many unable to function on basic levels. While Danny Whizz-Bang is able to display some semblance of normality, his violent, panic-stricken outbursts ultimately lead to his undoing. Barney Thompson is also prone to losing self-control, but languishes in an asylum for the insane. The experiences of both characters reflect the difficulties faced by ex-soldiers living with the disorder after the war and into the 1920s. With medical understanding still evolving, treatment ranged from extended rest to electro-convulsive therapy, while in acute cases many simply struggled to survive.

For those who lived with the consequences, from sufferers to family and friends like Tommy Shelby and Freddie Thorne, shell-shock was a cruel example of the psychological horrors of war. It could attract both sympathy and social stigma, and sentenced those living with the symptoms to a lifelong personal battle.

From a modern perspective, the experiences of the First World War soldiers diagnosed as shell-shocked opened the gateway for research into the effects of blasts on the human brain. It also served as a stepping stone in our understanding and recognition of Post-Traumatic Stress Disorder along with the development of appropriate treatment.

SHOES

'Never had shoes myself.'

Tommy's barefoot upbringing, along with his brothers, is central to the Shelby drive to make a name for themselves. As well as making bold moves in business, legitimate or otherwise, they dress to reflect their success, earn respect and command attention.

In terms of footwear, the early days of the Peaky Blinders in the dirty streets of Small Heath demanded heavy boots. As Tommy's ambitions grow, and take him to boardrooms, grand houses, hotels and even Parliament, so he switches to smart shoes in keeping with the era and reflecting a level of cool assurance.

The 1920s saw the Oxford shoe become a popular choice in both Great Britain and America, and it remains that way today. It's distinguished by a closed lacing system, in which the eyelets sit underneath the vamp, or front section, of the shoe. When laced and tied, the quarters (which host the eyelets) are pulled close, which leaves only the top of the tongue visible. With a low heel, the resulting smooth, streamlined shape makes these shoes as elegant to look at as they are comfortable to wear.

Throughout the decade, as the Oxford grew in popularity, so variations evolved from the plain, black leather model. Different colours came into play, often contrasting in the same shoe, such as brown, tan and oxblood, as well as material like suede. The cap toe became a mainstay, featuring a stitched band over the top of the shoe at the front. The brogue also emerged as a fashionable touch, this being a term used to describe a shoe like the Oxford with decorative elements such as patterned perforations.

The Derby is another popular shoe among the Peaky Blinders when they're dressed to kill. In contrast to the Oxford, it's defined by the fact that the eyelets are stitched to the outside of the vamp of the shoe. This is known as open lacing as opposed to the Oxford's closed system, so the eyelets remain on display once tied. The Derby was often favoured over the Oxford, as the lacing allowed a roomier fit. It was also a style that extended to boots with a smart, military look.

SIGNET RING

'Don't fuck with the Peaky Blinders.'

Attention to detail is important to the Shelby family, not just in business but in their dress sense. For the Peaky Blinders, the baker's boy cap, greatcoats, suits and boots might make an important first impression, but it is accessories like the watch chain and pocket square that demonstrate they're a cut above the rest.

Then there's the jewellery – specifically the kind of heavy-duty ring worn by Tommy, Arthur, John and even young Finn, which has served as a vital means of stamping an identity through the ages. With its flat, engraved top, intended to be dipped in a hot wax or soft clay seal, the signet ring doesn't just make a mark on documentation. For a Peaky Blinder, it also packs a punch when fists fly.

The signet ring is a functional item that has gone on to become a fashion mainstay. Worn on the little (pinkie) finger or the index finger, it's been called upon for thousands of years as a means of identification. With a unique engraving on the head, from a meaningful symbol to initials or a job title, military rank or family crest, the wearer could employ their signet ring to seal correspondence with a unique stamp.

Used since the earliest civilisations, and at times when reading and writing were not in widespread use, the signet ring seal often eclipsed the signature as a recognised sign of authority. Bearing a stamp of such personal meaning, and worn for life, it was originally destroyed on the death of the owner to prevent misuse. Over time, however, as the value of the material used to make the signet ring increased, it came to be considered as an heirloom to be passed down through the generations. While the origins of the Shelby brothers' signet rings are unknown, it's likely that in a family with such a strong sense of heritage these would be inherited items worn with great pride.

Larger than standard rings, and often made from precious metal such as gold or silver, the signet was considered to be a symbol of wealth and class. Anyone of standing, from kings and noblemen to politicians, lawyers and physicians, wore a signet ring to symbolise their importance, and over time this encouraged others to aspire to wear one. During the nineteenth century, incorporating semi-precious jewels such as ruby or sapphire, the ring became such a prized possession it was sometimes worn to display from the fob of a pocket watch. By then, the signet ring was no longer widely used as a means of sealing documents, but even as a decorative item its history signified that wearers took pride in their identity.

By the time the Peaky Blinders are forging their reputation in the 1920s, the sleek and sharp-edged style of the Art Deco movement lent itself comfortably to signet ring design. Over the last hundred years, the ring has even broken free from being a male preserve, with striking designs available for anyone who wishes to let their fingers do the talking.

THE SINGER FACTORY

'You're due at the Singer factory at eight tomorrow ... there's a union problem.'

Lizzie and Tommy, are not on good terms when she visits him at the Midland Hotel to brief him on his business agenda for the next day. While his personal life is troubled, he's grown to become a powerful businessman with interests in several Birmingham factories that were significant employers of the age.

The Singer Factory is a case in point. Established in Coventry in 1874 as a bicycle manufacturer, Singer would go on to build a reputation in the early twentieth century as a leading British car maker. The company operated from several sites, including one in Birmingham following the acquisition of land from BSA in 1926.

Singer continued to enjoy success as a motor manufacturer through the 1930s, and became closely linked with motorsport at that time including the Isle of Man TT and Le Mans 24 Hour Race. By the 1950s, however, the popularity of Singer cars was in decline, with the company ceasing production of their vehicles in 1970.

SLEEVE GARTERS

'You'd better show people you are still cocks of the walk.'

With his jacket slung over a chair, Tommy Shelby still manages to stay sharp and smart thanks to a small accessory that's been largely forgotten today.

A sleeve garter is a band worn over each arm of a shirt. Primarily, its function is to keep the sleeves out of any work that might get them messy. Ink is never far from Tommy's desk, for example, which meant a pair of sleeve garters didn't just look good but served a useful purpose.

In the 1920s, everyone from jazz pianists, speakeasy bartenders and gamblers adopted the sleeve garter in order to keep their hands free for the business at hand. With a history that dated back to the Wild West, where a sleeve garter would keep a shirt arm from interfering with a sharpshooter's gun draw, this was an accessory that came with a significant level of style.

As well as keeping a shirt clean, sleeve garters were also used to control the length of a sleeve when worn with a jacket. Strapped tight to each arm, it kept the shirt sleeve in the right place throughout the day. As attitudes relaxed towards formal dressing, so the sleeve garter fell out of fashion. Should shirt wearers find their cuffs got in the way, they simply rolled up their sleeves. Through the 1920s, however, when the Peaky Blinders made their name, this wasn't considered conventional. Then, shirt garters were a practical accessory that helped the Shelby brothers keep their sleeves out of trouble, whether they were counting

betting slips, penning letters or preparing for a
punch-up.

SMALL HEATH

*'When I drove into Small Heath, I thought I was going
to get murdered. Then I mentioned your name.'*

Horse trainer, aristocrat and widow, Lady May
Carleton is well aware that she looks out of place on
paying a visit to the Shelbys' Watery Lane betting
office. In 1922, it's no place for a lone woman who
dresses like she's worth a fortune, but she quickly
learns that she's safe on account of her association with
the Peaky Blinders.

Small Heath is the stomping ground for the Shelby
family. It's from their terraced house on Watery Lane,
just a stone's throw from the Garrison pub, that
Tommy, his brothers and their Aunt Polly set out to
build an underworld empire. Long before the Shelbys
strike it rich, and move out into grand country dwell-
ings, they establish themselves as lords of an urban
manor made up of grime-encrusted terraced streets,
factories that spit flames from furnaces, and canal-
side wharves and scrapyards. It might be down at heel
for a lady like May Carleton, but for the Peaky Blinders
it's a stronghold and a place they will always call home.

Small Heath today is a thriving multicultural
district in Birmingham, and largely unrecognisable
from the time when the Peaky Blinders reigned one
hundred years ago. Located to the south-east of the city
centre, the streets and cramped houses from the
Shelby era were mostly built in Victorian times to

accommodate factory workers. The BSA (Birmingham Small Arms Company) was one of the largest employers. Established on twenty-five acres of land on Armoury Road in Small Heath, the factory manufactured a range of goods, from machine-made firearms to bicycles and vehicles. By the turn of the twentieth century, Small Heath had become home to a large population of Irish immigrants, to which the Shelby family belonged.

By the 1920s, the canal running through Small Heath was in competition with the railways and roads as a transport route for industrial goods. Through much of the nineteenth century, however, factories and enterprises had located nearby, and the waterway thrived with their business. While activity on the canal through Small Heath had quietened considerably compared to the end of the nineteenth century, it suited the Peaky Blinders and their business interests. This is the location for Charlie Strong's yard and his narrowboat moorings, and a staging post for both the legitimate goods and the kind that Charlie will only transport for Tommy when there's no moon in the sky.

In the second half of the twentieth century, government regeneration schemes led to the demolition of many old slum houses to make way for modern developments. Small Heath today may be a far cry from the age of the Peaky Blinders, but its place in the mythology of the infamous street gang is assured for a long time to come.

ALF SOLOMON

'Every man, he craves certainty.'

Tom Hardy's Jewish gangster, Alfie Solomons, might seem like a unique fictional creation. In reality, his character is loosely inspired by a real-life underworld crime figure of the day, Alf Solomon.

Born in the mid-1890s to a Russian émigré mother, Solomon made his name as a volatile leader of a Jewish gang involved in bootlegging, gambling rackets and racecourse protection. Operating out of Camden in north London, he formed a close but uneasy allegiance with Clerkenwell-based nightclub owner Charles 'Darby' Sabini, who was himself fighting with Billy Kimber for control of racecourses across the south of England. The pact duly put Solomon at odds with Kimber's Birmingham Boys. Following a shooting outside Sabini's flat in 1921, it even led to Solomon standing trial for attempting to murder the Midlands mob boss. The case reportedly ended with Solomon's acquittal when no witness could recall the incident. Later that decade, Alf Solomon would return to the dock. Following a fracas at the Eden Social Club, he was found not guilty of the attempted murder of a doorman, but guilty of the murder of a patron, Buck Emden, and sent to prison for three years.

In 1936, Alf Solomon and his gang were believed to have joined with other Jewish groups, anarchists, communists and socialists in resisting Sir Oswald Mosley's British Union of Fascists at what became known as The Battle of Cable Street. In his later years,

Solomon reportedly tried to leave his violent gangster life behind him. He wrote a somewhat desperate letter to the police, offering to become an informant in return for protection from what he believed to be a mortal threat from rival gangs. Little is known of Alf Solomon's fate, though his life has now been immortalised as one of Britain's most memorable underworld players.

THE SUFFRAGE MOVEMENT

'You know the name of suffragettes? I'm impressed.'

It was one of the first social and political upheavals of the twentieth century in Britain, with consequences that impacted on the world of the Peaky Blinders and that still resonate today. In 1919, by the time Tommy Shelby finds himself in possession of stolen machineguns, the action taken by the suffragettes had arguably achieved their primary aim, though at huge personal costs. One year earlier, for the first time in British history, women had been allowed to vote at a General Election. As a result, there's no doubt that the legacy of the sacrifices made by women such as Emmeline Pankhurst empowers every female character in the story of *Peaky Blinders*, from family matriarchs like Polly Gray and Esme Shelby, to those determined to further the fight for equality such as union activist Jessie Eden. As for Tommy and his view of the cause, when he mentions the name of one of the most notable suffragettes over dinner, Jessie cautiously acknowledges that their values may be more aligned than she first thought.

Since the 1860s, voices had been calling for women's right to vote, but with little success. At a time when the establishment view was that women would not understand the complexities of Parliament, and with other female emancipation campaigns committed to peaceful debate and reasoning, such voices were largely ignored.

The Women's Social and Political Union was established in 1903 by a young activist called Emmeline Pankhurst and her two daughters. The union was borne of frustration at the status quo and pledged to take direct action in order to express its views. Dedicated to 'deeds, not words', the Pankhursts quickly attracted both support from activists, prepared to undertake radical steps in the name of the cause, and press attention.

Over the next ten years, the WSPU – dubbed 'the suffragettes' – earned a reputation for increasingly bold, disruptive action that frequently led to prison sentences. During this period, activists went from smashing shop windows and cutting telegraph wires to arson and even planting bombs. Their aim was to maintain maximum exposure, regardless of the law, while focusing their effort on damaging property without causing harm to people. Perhaps the most shocking and notable protest was undertaken by suffragette Emily Davison, who threw herself in front of the king's horse at the Epsom Derby in 1913 and died of her injuries. With suffragettes staging hunger strikes behind bars, leading to force-feeding by prison authorities, the public and political mood towards the movement became increasingly divided.

In some ways, the commencement of the First World War in 1914 proved to be a game-changer for the suffragettes. As hostilities broke out, and men signed up to fight, Emmeline Pankhurst encouraged women to halt their protests and get behind the war effort by taking on male roles left empty at home. Although some leading figures in the movement pledged to maintain their militant actions, notably Emmeline's daughter, Sylvia, this switch in focus only encouraged empathy for the cause and a final push towards the tipping point for electoral reform.

In 1918, just months before the end of the war, Parliament passed the Representation of the People Act. This gave the vote to women over the age of thirty – on condition that they were a member or married to a member of the Local Government Register – and while this did not provide equality with men (who could vote at twenty-one), it increased the electorate by nearly eight and a half million. The reforms were embraced by women with enthusiasm at the General Election later that year, in which they were also allowed to stand for the first time as MPs, and saw David Lloyd George's coalition return to power by a landslide.

One year later, as Tommy seeks to outmanoeuvre Chief Inspector Campbell in his bid to stamp out the Peaky Blinders, women were enjoying a newfound sense of empowerment across society. While the actions of the suffragettes had been viewed as borderline terrorism in some quarters, it led to the start of electoral reforms, with women being given the same right as men to vote aged twenty-one in 1928.

Ultimately, the Suffrage Movement paved the way for feminism to grow, challenge societal values and continue the fight for equality. When Linda Shelby encourages Polly, Esme and the women of Shelby Company Limited to stage a walk out in solidarity with Jessie Eden's strike for equal pay, they do so with the spirit of the Pankhursts still fresh in their minds. Whatever Tommy Shelby makes of it, even he recognises this is one unstoppable force for change.

SUIT

'Oh, I don't pay for suits. My suits are on the house, or the house burns down.'

With the exception of Tommy Shelby's view on the matter, a well-fitted, tailored suit can be a considerable financial investment. Then again, it's a wardrobe item that looks the part at any time or place, rising above fleeting fashion trends and providing lasting value for money at every level.

For the Peaky Blinders, the suit is central to their uniform. The traditional three-piece, comprising of jacket, trousers and waistcoat, is a mainstay for the Shelby brothers and Michael Gray. Even Aunt Polly lives up to her role as the family matriarch in a stunning grey ensemble, complete with aviator glasses, leather gloves and fedora hat.

In the first decade of the twentieth century, the suit we recognise today began to eclipse the frock coat. This knee-length jacket was the mainstay of men's fashion through both the Victorian and Edwardian era, but went into decline before the First World War. By the time soldiers returned from the frontline, the lounge or business suit had become acceptable attire. Even if the jacket didn't match the trousers, almost every man had a two- or three-piece they could call upon at the very least for Sunday best. For working-class men with aspirations like Tommy Shelby and his brothers, a well-made suit was a way to signify confidence, success and a willingness to do business on their terms.

Styles have changed in terms of lapel design or buttoning points, for example, but essentially the basic suit shape has remained the same since the early twentieth century. In the 1920s, soon after the end of the First World War, the suit was cut trim like a military uniform, before later moving towards the more generous blade suit of the 1930s, complete with broader, boxy shoulders and a tighter waist.

The fashion for dark, earthy or charcoal-coloured suits in the 1920s was largely down to the fact that these didn't show up the dirt and soot too quickly. This allowed for flashes of colour from either the tie or the pocket square. Heavy, course fabrics were the order of the day, such as wool or tweed, with single- or double-breasts and three to four buttons at the front, and lapels that grew wider towards the end of the decade. Tommy also has a blue suit in his wardrobe, which can only help him stand out from the crowd in terms of colour alone. It's a bold and stylish move, and suggests a man who can afford more than one suit.

Finally, there's the signature waistcoat of the age buttoned high across the chest to complement the penny collar shirt visible above. The waistcoat is effectively the third piece in a three-piece suit, and has been a fashion item for men since the seventeenth century. By the 1900s, it was no longer seen as finery but as workday clothing, and yet from the 1950s the waistcoat was once more the preserve of the well-dressed man. Back in the day of the Peaky Blinders, it's the overall package that sets them apart from ordinary folk. When Tommy and his brothers step out wearing a three-piece and accessories – from the pocket watch to the pocket square – it signals a shared identity among a band of brothers who are going places.

For Tommy, tailoring is key. He takes great pride in wearing a suit that's made to fit, and it shows. A jacket that's too big can swamp a frame or leave the wearer's legs looking short, while a suit that's on the small side is both restricting to wear and looks awkward. A fitted suit features clean lines and a shaped waist, sitting comfortably on the shoulders while defining the chest and arms. The sleeves should be cut to just above the wrist, and show between a quarter and half an inch of shirt cuff. The trousers taper at the leg to sit on top of the shoe, providing enough length so they don't ride too high on sitting down. Not only should a well-tailored ensemble bring out the best in your appearance, it should also feel as comfortable as a second skin. Whether the Shelbys are drinking at the bar, working behind a desk, watching a horse race or a boxing match, or slugging it out with rivals, they never look out of place in a suit.

Get the fit

There are three options when it comes to choosing a suit: off the peg, made to measure and bespoke. Much depends on budget, of course, and the recognition that unless your suits are specially made by a tailor then you get what you pay for.

OFF THE PEG

This is the cheapest way to owning a suit. It's factory-made, in keeping with fashion, and ready to wear. At the same time, a suit purchased directly off the rack may not fit in all the right places. It's also likely to be manufactured from cheap or thin material that wears thin or goes saggy and baggy. If you're simply after an affordable fashionable suit that lasts for a season, however, and content with the fact that it's not unique, then off the peg is a quick and simple solution.

MADE TO MEASURE

This is the middle ground when it comes to buying a suit. It won't break the bank, but the fitting will feel more natural than a cheaper, off-the-peg ensemble. Made to measure involves a trip to the tailor but with less of the financial commitment that comes with a bespoke suit. Here, you'll be measured up and presented with a range of styles and fabrics, but the suit will be tailored from standard, pre-cut pieces and then finessed to fit your frame and build. A made-to-measure suit feels personalised and is a popular option for those who take pride in the way that they dress.

BESPOKE

This is the top choice when it comes to a suit that serves as your signature look. Bespoke means the suit is tailored from scratch especially for you, from the fitting to the fabrics, the stitching, the finishing and finer details, with no compromise on quality and craftsmanship. In terms of process, the consultations, fittings and tailoring of the suit can take several months. The finished product should look unique and feel entirely natural, adding a Shelby level of confidence and swagger.

A bespoke suit is the most expensive option, but it can prove to be a good investment. Many people who invest in a top-quality, hand-made suit that fits like a dream, find it transcends fashion and lasts them for decades.

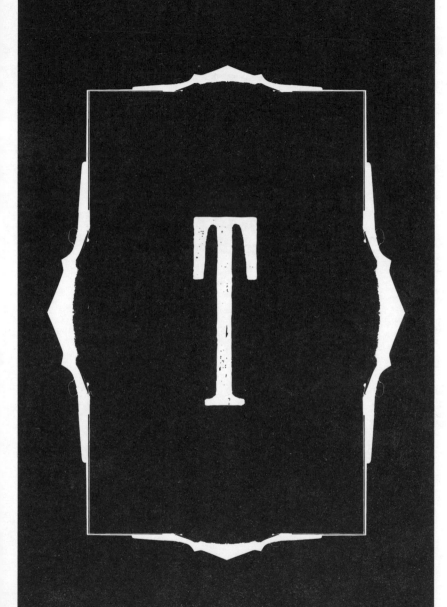

TIE

'Do I look like a man who wants a simple life?'

There is a time and place for a smart tie, as Tommy Shelby shows by example. At a time when the popular penny collar could be worn without any such accessory, and simply buttoned to the throat, an alternative shirt and tie caught the eye with a stripe of colour and fashion flare.

In many ways, Tommy and his brother in neckwear, Finn, were trailblazers when it came to the tie. Up until the 1920s, formal neckwear tended to be fussy, flowing, artfully folded items that had evolved from the cravat. The cloth scarf was a more popular accessory in terms of everyday accessories, and favoured by the working classes primarily to keep out the cold. Then came the modern tie. Seeking to make an item of neckwear that sat flush against the chest, New York tailor Jesse Langsdorf devised a new cut midway through the decade that took the world by storm. Smart, slim and simple to secure, the Langsdorf tie set the template for the tie as we know it, allowing men to express their creativity with colour. Later, in the 1930s as the fashion for ties exploded, the Duke of Windsor is said to have been responsible for the evolution of a larger knot that made the tie look fuller, known as the Windsor knot.

For Tommy Shelby, a good tie is about simplicity of shape and dark or muted colours. There's no call for flamboyant patterns or fancy knots here. This is a man whose character and actions command attention, with the devil in the detail, such as a simply folded pocket square or a tie knotted straight as a blade.

TIE BAR

'You're a fucking Shelby, so you're a general.'

Along with the pocket square and fob watch, this practical clip completes the holy trinity of Peaky Blinders suit accessories. It's all part of the uniform. Attaching the tie to the front of the shirt in order to keep it straight and neat, the tie bar is one more way Tommy sets an example to his troops – including Finn when he loses his way – by being impeccably presented no matter what the situation.

The tie bar evolved from the tie pin, which was a popular way to hold a cravat in place through the nineteenth century. With the advent of the modern tie, often made from light material such as silk, a weighted, sprung clip became a popular means of keeping the skinny end out of sight and stopping the whole thing from flapping and twisting around.

Tie bars can be made from a range of metals including silver and gold. They can be plain or ornate, and often engraved with company or club affiliations. In keeping with the simplicity of his wardrobe, when Tommy wears a tie bar it's as sleek as it is plain, but with the potential to catch the light and glint fiercely.

TOP HAT

'Love the hat, by the way.'

By the time Chief Inspector Campbell arrives in Birmingham, the top hat was well on the way to being knocked to the ground as everyday headwear. It had emerged in the late eighteenth century before rising to become the archetypal choice for upper-class gents through the Victorian age and on, into the Edwardian era. The top hat was originally made from beaver fur, pummelled into a felt and then cured with a mercury compound. When the toxic effects of the metal on the brain were established – which is how the term 'mad as a hatter' originated – silk, linen and shellac became common alternatives.

By 1919, as he approaches the secret service agents on the platform guarding Churchill's carriage, Campbell is a lone top-hat wearer in a crowd of flat caps and fedoras. Much of this was down to changing fashion, and the rise of more practical hats. Despite this, the all-familiar high-crown shape is much admired by the Secretary of State when Campbell boards the train to brief him, and it didn't drop out of view completely. Through the interwar years, the top hat returned to its roots as a symbol of the ruling classes. By the second half of the twentieth century, it had settled into place as the headwear of choice for funeral directors – worn with a black mourning band – and guests at special occasions such as racecourse days and weddings.

UMBRELLA

'You don't admit that. You say something like "umbrella mender". And we decide you're lying and arrest you.'

Inspector Moss is exasperated with the Digbeth Kid, a naive young man who has been paid by the Peaky Blinders to be 'stood up' to spend a week in jail for illegal betting activities. Moss has also been bought off by the gang. He knows the lad has done nothing wrong. In order to earn time behind bars, and so take the heat out of the Chief Inspector's investigations into Tommy Shelby and his associates, the Kid needs to at least provide Moss with a flimsy cover story for him to see through and then detain him. To this end, Moss prompts the Kid to claim he earns a living from a trade that would have attracted quite some demand in 1919.

With rain a central feature of the British landscape, the umbrella has played a role in British society since the eighteenth century. While originally regarded as a feminine accessory, with a handle and shaft fashioned from whalebone, and a canvas or oiled silk canopy, by the start of the nineteenth century it had been widely adopted by men as well, keen to protect their finery from a soaking.

At the turn of the twentieth century, the umbrella had become an everyday item for anyone who wished to stay dry in a downpour. The men's umbrella was generally wider in circumference than the counterpart for women, and also heavier, and yet both had moved on in terms of materials. An umbrella befitting a Peaky Blinder would typically feature a metal frame and ribs with a waterproof cotton canvas, and a handle made from antler, horn or carved wood, reflecting the bearer's status.

It wasn't until 1928 that the collapsible umbrella shook up the market. Until then, the umbrella was often used like a walking cane, and could prove sturdy enough to be employed as an effective weapon in the hands of a Shelby in a spot of bother.

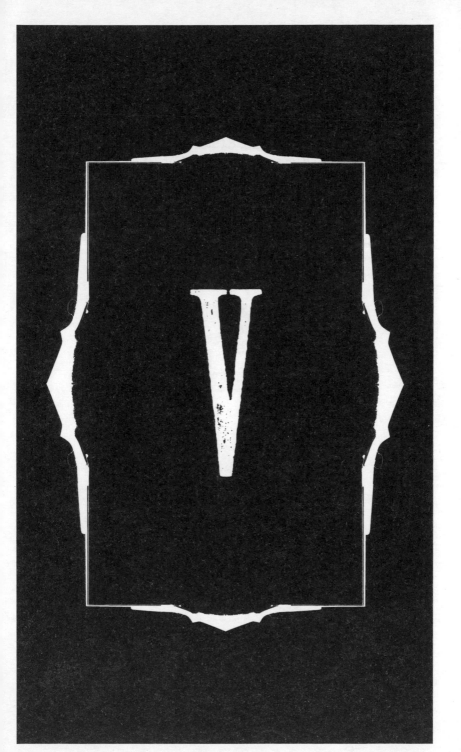

VARDO

'Tommy's gone! I swear to God he's in the wagon with Johnny Dogs.'

The Shelbys live a settled life, starting out in their Watery Lane terrace in Small Heath before graduating to town and manor houses, and yet they're never far from their Gypsy roots. On several occasions, Tommy returns to the familiar horse-drawn wagons (known as vardos) that were central to the Romani Traveller's way of life at the time. He seeks an audience in a wagon belonging to Zilpha Lee, seeking to settle a feud by arranging a marriage between kin. Later, grief-stricken following the murder of Grace via a bullet intended for him, he takes to the road in one with his old associate before Finn can alert the rest of the family. Most poignantly of all, the body of John Shelby is laid to rest inside a Gypsy wagon, along with his treasured personal items, and committed to a funeral pyre.

The brightly decorated wooden wagon commonly associated with Romani Travellers had, in fact, only been adopted by the community in Britain for approximately half a century prior to the time of the Peaky Blinders. Before that, Gypsy families travelled on foot or in tilted carts pulled by horses. While some were known to sleep under makeshift tents made from hazel branches drawn together and leashed under canvas (known as 'benders'), others bedded down in the carts or used them as shelter to sleep underneath. In France, Romanis had already merged the concept of the bender tent with the cart to give rise to the vardo (a word originating from Iran, meaning 'cart'). By the second half of the nineteenth century, the practice had crossed to the UK.

Hand crafted by specialist coach builders, using a seasoned timber frame such as oak or walnut, and adorned with intricate paintwork and carvings, the vardo earned a reputation as a work of folk art on wheels. Often bow-topped, but built in a variety of styles, a vardo ranged from basic living to comparative luxury, but always with the freedom to move on. A cast-iron stove with fireplace and chimney was incorporated into some designs, providing warmth and a means of cooking as well as shelter for travelling families. Creative use of space meant cupboard and storage space was available alongside berths for both adults and children. Above all, the careful attention to decoration and detail invested in each vardo became a source of pride for the owner and an integral part of Romani life as they rolled into the twentieth century.

Despite the prevalence of the vardo across the British countryside in the first few decades of the 1900s, their use went into decline from the 1930s, in contrast with the rise in popularity of the motor vehicle.

VEHICLES

'There's a fucking great Riley parked out there, with nobody watching it!'

In 1922, a prestigious vehicle like the one May Carleton has left outside the Shelbys' betting shop would have been a rare and unusual sight. She's arrived to meet Tommy at a time when a transport revolution had only just got underway, with cars produced for a mass market beginning to squeeze the horse and cart off the road.

It had been just under thirty years since the first

motor car was driven on British roads. In that time, since 1895, the number of vehicles had risen steeply from just fifteen in the first year to almost one thousand at the turn of the century. Over the next three decades, car ownership rose exponentially. The first sight of a vehicle in Watery Lane takes place in 1919, as Tommy collects Grace from outside the Garrison and drives her to a day at the races. Crank-started by Charlie Strong, and maintained by Curly – who prefers horses because he can talk to them – the English Ford Model T doesn't just turn Grace's head. While car ownership was growing at the time, it's still a relative novelty in a poor quarter like Small Heath.

As the Peaky Blinders expand their business interests and go from strength to strength, so their choice of cars reflects their success. From 1919 to 1922, and 1925 to 1929, Tommy and his family get behind the wheel of all manner of increasingly impressive vehicles, from the popular Austin 12/4 to the prowling Bentley 3 Litre Vanden Plas and the luxurious Daimler Straight 8 4.5 Litre. By the end of the decade, the motoring landscape had changed beyond recognition, with almost one million cars on the road in Britain.

VODKA

'I think tonight you should not drink vodka with your champagne.'

When Tommy tangles with Tatiana and the Russian exiles, he finds that vodka is the drink they rely upon to toast every occasion and to cause guards to drop when they're needed most. Faced with a princess who has designs on him in several ways, his advice to her is treated with amusement and intrigue. For the princess, raised in a culture of hard drinking, vodka allows her to gain the upper hand in both business and pleasure.

In the 1920s, vodka was a comparatively new import into Britain. Following the Russian Revolution and the end of the First World War a year later, it was largely introduced here by those fleeing westward from countries that considered vodka to be their national drink.

Vodka is a largely flavourless but strong alcoholic drink that's traditionally made from distilling fermented grain. A strong homebrew culture established itself in Russia in the early years of the twentieth century, using potatoes in place of corn, wheat or rye, often giving rise to vodka with dangerously high levels of alcohol by volume. In 1917, following the Revolution, the state took over production and distribution of the drink. From there, thanks to fleeing aristocrats such as the Romanovs in *Peaky Blinders*, Russia began to set the standard as the vodka of choice around the world.

American drinkers had to wait for the end of Prohibition before they could truly find out what the fuss was all about. This was mostly down to bartenders returning home from Europe, where they had sought employment in high-end hotels during the USA's failed experimentation with teetotalism. While those with Russian or Polish heritage traditionally drank vodka neat and without ice, the West recognised its potential as a mixer. As a result, through the 1930s and into the 1940s, vodka established itself alongside traditional spirits such as whiskey, gin, brandy and rum as a drink in its own right and as an essential base spirit for popular cocktails of the age such as the Bloody Mary, Moscow Mule and Long Island Iced Tea.

WALL STREET CRASH

'I told Michael on Friday that this was going to happen.'

The phone rings in the Shelby Company Limited's Detroit office. Michael Gray is out cold on the sofa. Half-empty glasses and clothing lie discarded on the floor, along with a gun and the sleeping form of Michael's underwear-clad, soon-to-be-fiancée, Gina. Finally, Michael stirs and takes the call. He does not like what he hears about the value of the company's considerable investments, and confirms the worst on reading the ticker-tape machine spooling very bad news indeed.

It's Tuesday 29 October 1929, the dawn of the greatest stock market calamity in history.

The Wall Street Crash began towards the end of the previous week, though it had been brewing for some time. In this last year of the decade, known as the Roaring Twenties, the American economy had enjoyed a period of unprecedented growth. It was a time of great confidence in future prosperity as mass markets opened, urban populations expanded and cities grew upwards. Drawn to the returns, companies and everyday speculators began investing heavily on the stock market. Many borrowed money to buy stock, while ignoring growing concern that overproduction and a reliance on credit issued by the country's numerous banks were unsustainable.

Eventually, in the autumn of 1929, investors could no longer ignore the warning signs. With sales down and debt rising, sectors such as agriculture and construction were beginning to contract. A sell-off in stocks started to develop in September, which soon impacted on their prices. As values reduced, brokers were instructed to dump stock by clients who feared they wouldn't be able to meet loan repayments. By late October, a rising sense of unease gripped Wall Street in New York, which is where the American stock exchange is located. On Thursday 24 October, like a retreating ocean before a tsunami, some thirteen million shares were traded with diminishing values.

At the end of the following day, known as Black Friday, the market closed trading for the week having recovered somewhat. Many investors believed the worst was over, but Tommy Shelby was not among that number. Wise to the rising sense of economic crisis across the Atlantic that day, Tommy instructs Michael – the company's representative in America – to sell off their investments with immediate effect. Tommy's bullish young cousin secretly decides to overrule him and follow his broker's advice to hold on. Having lived the high life over a long weekend, the first Michael learns of the economic disaster that has swept away the value of the Shelby Company's investments is when his office phone rings on what became known as Black Tuesday.

The Wall Street Crash sent economic shockwaves around the world. It sparked the beginning of the Great Depression, with America at the epicentre, which would last for ten years until the outbreak of the Second World War. In the USA, as everyday citizens had become investors, people lost their homes and jobs while businesses were rendered worthless at a stroke. In the world of the Peaky Blinders, the crash forces Tommy to refocus his efforts on daring criminal dealings in order to save Shelby Company Limited and ensure it continues to thrive.

WHISKEY

'Whiskey is good proofing water. It tells you who's real and who isn't.'

When Tommy Shelby reflects on the qualities of whiskey with the new Garrison barmaid, Grace Burgess, he's about to discover that as an undercover agent of the crown she hopes to share the same ability to disarm.

Throughout the story of the Peaky Blinders, this is a drink that's never far from reach. Tommy and his brothers are so familiar with the spirit that they know a good bottle when they see one, and the sense of courage or comfort it can bring. In keeping with the Shelby family's roots, however, it has to be Irish in origin. Scotch whisky (spelled with no 'e') or simply known as 'Scotch'? That's for smuggling to Prohibition America hidden in crates of car parts.

Made from fermented barley or grains, the resulting spirit has been a popular drink across Britain since the fifteenth century. Scotland and Ireland soon became established producers, distilling and refining Scotch and Irish whiskey respectively by each using a distinct approach to the process. With two filled glasses placed on the bar, a Peaky Blinder could differentiate between them at a glance as much as a taste. Here's how to know one from the other:

Scotch whisky

As a rule, a Scotch whisky is made from malted barley – or with the addition of grain – and distilled twice. Different varieties are available, from the popular single malt or grain (which means it's made at one distillery) to blended malt, blended grain and blended Scotch whisky. Finally aged in oak barrels for at least three years, Scotch can have a distinctively earthy, fiery taste and darker colour than its Irish counterpart.

Irish whiskey

Typically made from unmalted barley or grain, the most distinguishing feature of an Irish whiskey is the fact that in general it's distilled three times. After being aged in oak barrels for a minimum of three years, the resulting spirit has a light quality with a smooth finish and paler colour than Scotch. There are four different types of Irish whiskey. The blended variety – often considered the most popular – single malt, single grain and single pot still, which means it also includes malted barley in the distillation process.

The debate about whether Irish whiskey or Scotch is superior continues to this day. Both are high-quality spirits with a rich heritage. Tommy and his brothers might have a preference, but quite literally it comes down to taste.

WILDERNESS HOUSE

'The day is my own. Good. I will walk around the maze, which is no longer confusing.'

A butler hurries across pristine walled gardens towards a grand building. He's carrying a breakfast tray and his pace suggests that whoever awaits him has exacting demands. Sure enough, when he sets the tray at the table of Grand Duke Leon Petrovich Romanov, his late arrival is met with nothing but criticism. The butler then goes through the duke's itinerary, who is quietly stung by the empty day that yawns ahead of him, but for a business appointment with one Thomas Shelby. For this is a man who has experienced nothing but attention and privilege throughout his life in Russia, until being forced to flee during the Revolution. Now, by invitation of the king, the duke resides with his family at a grace-and-favour house in Hampton Court.

As exiles, the duke, his wife and niece, Princess Tatiana Petrovna, live a gilded life in a majestic residence close to the Thames called Wilderness House. Nothing, it seems, can spoil their intention to take advantage of the king's generosity, until Tommy Shelby pays a visit with designs of his own.

Away from the world of the Peaky Blinders, Wilderness House is a real address that forms part of London's Hampton Court Palace estate. It's believed to have been built around 1700 to accommodate the Palace's Master Gardener. Most notably among those in the role who took up residence over the centuries was the famous landscape architect, 'Capability'

Brown. The house became a grace-and-favour residence in the late nineteenth century, with extensive renovations carried out – including electricity in 1907 – before accommodating its most celebrated aristocratic occupant thirty years later, the Grand Duchess Xenia of Russia, sister of Tsar Nicholas II.

X IS FOR A CROSS IN A BOX

BALLOTING PAPER

Election of the member of Parliament of the Birmingham South Constituency

*Vote for **only one candidate** by putting a cross in the box next to your choice*

1	CARR, Ronald	Conservative	1	◯
2	HALL, Bernard	Liberal	2	◯
3	ROSS, Michael	Communist	3	◯
4	SHELBY, Thomas	Labour	4	⊗

YEOMANRY

'I spent a long time waiting for the cavalry, me.'

In *Peaky Blinders*, Tommy, Arthur and John fought during the First World War as soldiers in the Warwickshire Yeomanry. This was one of fifty-five Yeomanry regiments in the British Army when the conflict began, which traditionally served as support to the cavalry. Like Tommy Shelby himself, Yeomanry soldiers have a close association with horses. Not all fought on horseback during the First World War, however, with many serving as foot-soldiers as part of the Royal Warwickshire Regiment.

Tommy, Arthur and John, and several of their local Peaky Blinders associates including Jeremiah Jesus, Danny Whizz-Bang and Freddie Thorne, were grouped together as The Small Heath Rifles. Populating regiments with volunteers from the same neighbourhood or area was part of a system that aimed to promote loyalty among men who had enlisted together. It was subsequently abandoned during the war, however, when heavy losses forced regroupings.

Based on his distaste for Turkish cigarettes, it's likely that Arthur fought with the Warwickshire Yeomanry at Gallipoli between 1915 and 1916. A disaster for the Allies, a large number of troops were subsequently redeployed to France to bolster numbers there. At some stage during their long service on the Western Front, Tommy, Danny and Freddie become tunnellers. This was highly dangerous work that earned huge respect from other soldiers. Tunnellers played a significant role supporting the Allies in the 1917 Battle of the

Somme, and Tommy's efforts in *Peaky Blinders* earn him promotion to the highest level under officer class.

On several occasions in the *Peaky Blinders* storyline, the Shelby brothers show nothing but disdain for cavalry officers. According to one account that Tommy gives of his wartime experience, an appeal for their help by his brigade, while facing certain death at the hands of the enemy, earned an unforgivably slow response. Tommy claims that when the cavalry finally arrived, one officer revealed he had been delayed in order to complete a game of cards. Appalled, Tommy shoots him in the head and reports him for cowardice.

ZOOT SUIT

'What the fuck is that racket?'

Arthur feels like a stranger in a new and unfamiliar world when the Peaky Blinders walk into Charles 'Darby' Sabini's Eden Club for the first time. The dancefloor is a riot of pretty young women cavorting in shockingly short dresses and boys who are dressed to kill. Many openly snort cocaine at the tables, and brazenly indulge in sexual activity, while a black jazz trio on stage pump out a frantic beat. They're dressed identically, in smart, angular and tapered drape suits that were set to evolve in the 1930s into a distinct outfit embraced by Afro-American and Latino hipsters.

With a high waist band, pegged trousers and a long coat with broad, padded shoulders, the zoot suit first emerged in America in the early 1930s. Supposedly named after an African-American slang word for 'suit', the distinctive tapering from top to bottom set the outfit apart from all others with the sense of flow it created. The pocket watch became a popular accessory once more, but this time with an exaggerated length to the chain, while many took to finishing the ensemble with a brimmed hat.

Popular in cities with strong African-American communities, such as New York, Detroit and Chicago, the zoot suit soon became a style item for young black men in particular who were seeking to make a bold statement. Enthusiasts included the big band leader Cab Calloway, and the singer Louis Armstrong, and their influence led to a strong association through the 1930s and 40s between the zoot suit and the jazz scene.

The suit even attracted criticism for its excessive use of cloth material, which was viewed as wasteful in some quarters and interpreted by others as a reflection of prejudice towards minority interests. The civil rights leader, Malcolm X, is said to have bought one on credit as a younger man, which reflected the high cost of the suit at the time as much as the powerful sense of assertiveness it created.

Fashion left the zoot style behind in the 1950s, but the suit continued a journey that started in the eighteenth century, defined a Birmingham street gang and remains a signature outfit for so many to this day.

An invitation from the publisher

Join us at www.hodder.co.uk, or follow us
on Twitter @hodderbooks to be a part of
our community of people who love the very
best in books and reading.

Whether you want to discover more about a book
or an author, watch trailers and interviews, have the
chance to win early limited editions, or simply browse
our expert readers' selection of the very best books,
we think you'll find what you're looking for.

And if you don't, that's the place to tell us what's missing.

We love what we do, and we'd love you to be a part of it.

www.hodder.co.uk

@hodderbooks

HodderBooks

HodderBooks